Mutual Tuition and Moral Discipline; Or, Manual of Instructions for Conducting Schools Through the Agency of the Scholars Themselves

Bates

Mutual Tuition

1823

56475

(handwritten notations, illegible)

Arthur Ransom

MUTUAL TUITION

AND

MORAL DISCIPLINE;

OR,

𝔐anual of 𝔍nstructions

FOR CONDUCTING SCHOOLS

THROUGH THE AGENCY OF THE SCHOLARS THEMSELVES.

SEVENTH EDITION.

For the Use of Schools and Families.

WITH AN

INTRODUCTORY ESSAY ON THE OBJECT AND IMPORTANCE

OF THE

𝔐adras 𝔖ystem of 𝔈ducation;

A BRIEF EXPOSITION OF THE PRINCIPLE ON WHICH IT IS FOUNDED;

AND A HISTORICAL SKETCH OF ITS RISE, PROGRESS, AND RESULTS.

BY THE REV. ANDREW BELL, D.D. LL.D.

F. As. S.: F. R. S. Ed.: PREBENDARY OF WESTMINSTER; AND MASTER OF
SHERBURN HOSPITAL, DURHAM.

"Moses chose able men out of all Israel, and made them heads over the people,
rulers of thousands, rulers of hundreds, rulers of fifties, and rulers of tens."—
EXODUS xviii. 25.

"Sicut firmiores in literis profectus alit æmulatio: ita incipientibus atque adhuc
teneris, condiscipulorum quam præceptoris, jucundior, hoc ipso quod facilior,
imitatio est."—QUIN.

LONDON:

PRINTED FOR G. ROAKE, 31, STRAND,

C. & J. RIVINGTON, ST. PAUL'S CHURCH YARD; HATCHARD AND
SON, PICCADILLY; W. BLACKWOOD, EDINBURGH;
AND J. CUMMING, DUBLIN.

1823.

Printed by R. CLAY, Devonshire-street,
Bishopsgate, London.

TO

THE NATIONAL SOCIETY,

THE DIOCESAN, CO-OPERATING,

AND

AUXILIARY SOCIETIES,

FOR THE EDUCATION OF THE POOR,

&c. &c. &c.

𝕿𝖍𝖊𝖘𝖊 𝕴𝖓𝖘𝖙𝖗𝖚𝖈𝖙𝖎𝖔𝖓𝖘,

FOR THE USE OF THEIR SCHOOLS,

ARE RESPECTFULLY DEDICATED,

BY THEIR FAITHFUL, HUMBLE SERVANT,

THE AUTHOR.

Contents.

	Page
INTRODUCTION.—§ 1, On the Object, Importance, Results, and Bearings of the Madras System of Education	1
§ 2.—On its Organ, or distinctive Principle................	16
§ 3.—On the subordinate Practices of the New School	19
§ 4.—To Parents, and to Institutors and Preceptors of Village Schools	22*
§ 5.—On the Instruction of the whole Poor Population	23*

PART I.

Sketch of Discovery, Promulgation, and Diffusion of the New or Madras System.

CHAP. I.—On the Discovery of " A System of Tuition altogether New"	21
II.—On the Promulgation of the New System of Education in India	26
III.—On the publication of the Madras System of Education in London, and on its introduction into English Schools....	28
IV.—On the general Diffusion of the Madras System in its genuine simplicity; and with it of the Gospel of Peace and Salvation; and on its tendency to the speedy Fulfilment of the Prophecies............................	30
V.—On the Partial Diffusion of the Madras System under different appellations, particularly under the denomination of Lancasterian	36
VI.—On the Primary Testimony of Mr. Lancaster to the Authenticity and Originality of the Madras System, confronted with Extracts from the Madras Reports, 1789-96, and Mr. Lancaster's " Improvements," 1st, 2d, and 3d editions, 1803, 1805, &c.	38
VII.—On Mr. Lancaster's Retraction of his preceding Acknowledgments; on his Claim to the Discovery of Mutual Tuition: and on the Testimony of his Friends and Advocates on that head	46
VIII.—Further Documents corroborative of those already quoted, and of the Facts which have been stated, relative to the Origin of the Madras System, to its Character, and Results, and to the continuation of the History to the present Time	50
IX.—Continuation of the Official Documents and Vouchers under the hands of the highest Authorities—Recapitulation and Conclusion—Royal Military and Naval Asylums and Schools — the Barrington School—and the National Society	52

Page

PART II.

On the Madras System of Education.

CHAP. I.—Object of Elementary Education............... 57

II.—Scheme of a School on the Madras or National System.. 58

III.—On the Classification of a School 59

IV.—On the Discipline of a School—its Rewards and Punishments 62

V.—On Perfect Instruction and Order 67

VI.—On the Master and Teachers 70

PART III.

On the Practices of the Madras School, or the Methods pursued in the Application of Mutual Tuition to a course of Elementary Education.

CHAP. I.—On the Course of Study 77

II.—On Writing and Transcribing 81

III.—On Simultaneous Instruction in Reading and Writing—on Sand — on Slate—an alphabetical series of Vowels and Consonants 86

IV.—On Monosyllabic Reading—by Pauses and Clauses...... 92

V.—On Promiscuous Reading Lessons—Syllabic Reading—unreiterated Spelling.............................. 97

VI.—On Morality and Religion 103

VII.—On Arithmetic, in a series of consecutive lessons 110

VIII.—On Economy 121

IX.—On Registers, and Weekly Examinations............. 123

X.—On Schools — for the richer Classes of the Community, and higher Branches of Study—Grammar and Classical—Ladies'—and Schools of Industry—Valediction 126

POSTSCRIPT. — § 1. Original Pupils of Madras Asylum. § 2. Original School Committee of National Society. § 3. Bishop Porteus's Pastoral Letter, and Negro Slaves. § 4. Native School of African Negro. § 5. Conclusion of Instructions for Conducting Regimental Schools. § 6. Valedictory Request 130

GENERAL INDEX

Of principal points, recommended to the particular consideration of Managers and Visitors of Schools;—the observance of which will correct or prevent the frequent errors, and consequent failures of Preceptors,—and will most effectually advance the happiness and improvement of the pupils.

1. *Classification.*—Let the Master arrange the School into classes, by allowing every child to find his level, p. 58, 60; and continually feed the higher classes from the lower. p. 60-1.

2. *Teachers.*—Select, qualify, direct, and superintend the teachers, and instruct their classes as often as is necessary. p. 70-7.

3. *Order, Regularity, and Quietness.*—Teach the children to observe the utmost order, regularity, and quietness, in every act, and every movement, in their daily entering and leaving school, taking their seats at the desks and on the benches, and their places in their classes on the floor, p. 67; and let them at once be trained to form their classes orderly into three sides of a square (or segment of a circle), preserving equal distances from one another. p. 60.

4. *Distinct and audible Reading.*—It is of the utmost consequence that every child learn to speak audibly, slowly, and distinctly. The neglect of this important rule is a perpetual source of inaccuracy, hindrance, and annoyance, and often loses more than half the time spent in school. p. 87, 104.

5. Let every child repeat incessantly, in a low voice, whatever is read or rehearsed by his school-fellows. p. 68, 79.

6. Begin with any boy in the class indiscriminately, p. 95, and let a brisk circulation in reading and rehearsing keep alive the attention of every member of the class, in quick succession, pp. 80, 93-4, 100—102.

7. It is of great importance that the members of the class learn to prompt, and take places, as prescribed; without which emulation slumbers, the school no longer

resembles a bee-hive: and the Ludus Literarius, or game of letters, loses its earnestness, and main interest. This earnestness and interest are greatly checked, when the master or teacher, instead of requiring the boys to prompt and take places of their own accord — calls out *tell*, and more especially when he prompts himself: nor, on the other hand, must all the scholars be allowed to stretch out their necks, and bawl at once. This (like other faults) is prevented by the boys, who speak out of turn, forfeiting a place. pp. 61, 64.

8. From the beginning, let the children examine one another, at the end of every lesson, on the meaning of the words, and of the sentences, pp. 80, 99, 106—108.

9. Let reading and writing be carried on simultaneously. pp. 79, 81-2, 86, 88, &c.

10. Perfect instruction is a main and indispensable law. See pp. 67—70, 105.

11. Let the scholars be instructed to read the pages, contents of chapters, or sections, &c., and to turn to any page, section, chapter, and verse, &c., when required. pp. 94, 98, 99.

12. Let the child, on the day of admission into school, begin to learn by heart, and rehearse the Lord's Prayer, &c., and let a certain portion be exacted daily, and perfectly learned. pp. 68, 103-4.

13. Let him also, on the first day, enter on a course of arithmetic; which, after a little practice, he prosecutes of his own accord. pp. 110—120.

14. Once a week, before the hour of examination, let every copy, ciphering book, and slate (filled, on one side, with writing, and, on the other, with a sum in ciphering) be arranged round the desks, or benches, in order of the performance. pp. 84, 125.

15. In spelling off book, let the words be written while spelling; but let hard words only be spelt: and after a certain progress, it will seldom be necessary to spell more than one or two words in a lesson. p. 98.

16. The disregard of equal and impartial justice in administering the laws of the school is a fault, for which nothing can compensate or atone. *passim.*

" Mind these rules before you mend them."

Mutual Tuition & Moral Discipline.

INTRODUCTION.

It will be observed, that this preliminary Essay is addressed to the courteous Readers, who possess power and means of forwarding the object to which it is directed, rather than to the professional men, for whose use the subsequent Manual is chiefly intended. But it is hoped, that the Masters of the Schools for the Poor will, in passing through this Introduction to their Text-Book, lay hold of some observations or reflections, on the nature of the interesting and eventful office with which they are intrusted, that may animate them to the faithful and earnest exercise of their functions.

" I take schoolmasters to have a more powerful influence upon the spirits of men, than preachers themselves. Forasmuch as they have to deal with younger and tenderer minds, and, consequently, having the advantage of making the earliest and deepest impressions upon them; but to preach to people without principle, is to build where there is no foundation; or, rather, where there is not so much as *ground* to build upon."—SOUTH.

§ I. *On the object, importance, results, and bearings of the Madras System of Education; with an apology for the execution of a task imposed by the present state of things, and the circumstances of the times.*

" The first springs of great events, like those of mighty rivers, are often mean and little."—SWIFT.

To give weight and efficiency to the following *Manual for conducting Schools, through the agency of the Scholars themselves,* it is necessary to preface

b

it with a brief survey of this System of Education, from its origin to the present time. This is certainly the most important, and, it may be, the last, office which it is peculiarly incumbent on the Author to perform, in furtherance of the object of his long and earnest pursuits. He feels it a duty, above all others, imperative on him, once more to retrace the System of Mutual Tuition and Moral Discipline, to the spring from which it issued; to contemplate it in its source; and, keeping pace with the current of time, to follow the course of its streams, as they flow in every quarter of the globe, and are in progress, carrying with them the "knowledge of the Lord," to overspread the earth, " as the waters cover the sea."

This System has no parallel in scholastic history. It is essentially discriminated from all others by the inherent principle, which constitutes its natural, necessary, and never-to-be-confounded distinction. It also differs materially from them in the LAWS by which it is regulated, and in the practices which it employs.

Nor is it less strikingly distinguished by the results, which it has produced. Its success has been as remarkable, as its nature is popular. In a period, less than the computed age of man, (or one-third of a century) it has reached the remotest regions of the earth, and is making rapid advances towards universal diffusion. No Founder of any school, ancient or modern, ever lived to witness so wide a spread of his System.

To what cause can this be ascribed? Whence this sudden and unexampled *Epoch* in the scho-

lastic world? For such an effect, an adequate
cause, and the only adequate one, may be found
in the INTRINSIC CHARACTER OF THE SYSTEM
—THE NATURE AND UNIVERSALITY. OF THE
PRINCIPLE ON WHICH IT IS FOUNDED,—THE
FACILITY AND ECONOMY OF ITS EXECUTION,
— THE SINGULARITY AND IMMENSITY OF
ITS POWER.

Archimedes wanted ground on which to stand,
that, with his mechanical lever, he might move
the terraqueous globe. The intellectual lever,
now discovered, requires no new planet, no distinct fulcrum, on which to rest. The seat of its
power, and its operation, is equally in the infant
mind. Wherever the race of man is to be found,
there is the spot on which may be placed this
engine, that is not only capable of moving, but is
actually, by an infallible. and irresistible impulse,
giving motion to, the moral world.

Now, if this System possesses such incalculable
powers; if, as stands on the highest authority,
" it is fitted to give a new character to society at
large;"* how important must it be, that the movements of so mighty an engine be properly directed.
There is nothing so momentous, not to parents
only, but to the Prince, and to the people, as the
education: of children: No question so deeply
interesting, as—by what means the welfare of the
rising generation can be most effectually advanced

* Report of National Society, 1812, p. 19. See important
extracts to this effect from their Reports, p. 55—7 infra. See also
Elements of Tuition, Part I. p. 96—114, for interesting documents,
whence it will appear that this System actually did give *a new character* to the race of children, who were its original pupils.

—by what culture, under the Divine blessing, their intellectual, moral, and religious character can be raised to that degree of perfection, of which humanity is susceptible; — and with this view, above all, and before all, how the Gospel of Peace and Salvation can be most deeply implanted in the infant breast!

The Author, however strongly impressed with this view of the subject, apprehends, that in humbly offering a practical solution of the question just proposed, an apology may be due to those who do not enter into his feelings, when they are opposed to established usage, inveterate habits, and ancient authority;—1, *for the style in which he expresses his sentiments* ;—2, *for the egotism which occurs in 'the narrative;—and, 3, for the documents which are introduced to authenticate it.*

1. In apology for *the language* in which he attempts to describe the effects and consequences of the discovery which he had hit upon, he can only say, he has no words whereby he can adequately convey his sentiments of the System built on this discovery, which he verily believes to be an instrument more powerful than ever yet has been wielded by the Moralist or Divine, the Statesman or Politician, the Sovereign or Legislature.

2. The *narrative*, he trusts, carries its excuse with it.   The origin of this discovery, the measures subsequently pursued to promote its progress, and the success of those measures, are matters of historical record, which do not depend on uncertain testimony, or anonymous statements—facts that stand on the most irrefragable evidence, on which

any history, merely human, ever stood — facts which were recorded, in every stage of their progress, with every seal and stamp of authenticity. In relating these facts, " quorum pars magna *fuit*," egotism or personality is unavoidable, whenever the Author speaks of himself, or of what he has done, whether in the first, or in the third person.

3. In regard to the *documents and vouchers inserted in this volume*, he has to crave indulgence, when, in order to authenticate this singular history, he is under the necessity — a necessity imposed by circumstances well known — of *reproducing documents*, with which is intimately and inseparably blended so much that is personal, so much that *needeth* apology. It is not for the sake of barren and unprofitable truths, that *such vouchers* are inserted in this volume; it is in the hope, that a brief summary of incontrovertible facts, extracted from original sources, from official reports, and from the most venerable and respectable authorities, may at length remove all doubts, in every quarter, regarding the true character and real object of the Madras System: and thereby promote its adoption in schools for all ranks of the community, and accelerate the grand *consummation* for which it seems destined.

While the Author contemplates, with much complacency, the list of the illustrious personages, and distinguished characters, who have united their endeavours towards the completion of so desirable an object, he would spare no effort to add to the number of their coadjutors and fellow-labourers; and he even ventures *still* to indulge in the humble hope, (so frequently expressed in his former publications) " that the Legislature may be induced, in due time, to take measures to render effectual, secure, and permanent, to all the children of the state, that boon, which, under the gracious sanction of the Prince Regent, His Royal Highness the Commander-in-Chief bestowed on all the children of the army; and thereby to fulfil the benevolent wish of the FATHER OF HIS PEOPLE, by making legal provision, that all of them *may be taught, on an economical plan, to read their Bible, and understand the doctrines of our Holy Religion :*"

" Et reor, et, si quid veri mens augurat, opto."

·To those who have read any authentic Narrative of the rise and progress of the Madras System, or shall read the following sketch of its history, these apologetical observations may appear superfluous; for there it will be seen, that no pretensions are set up to any merit, either for the original discovery, or subsequent promulgation, the Author having always considered himself merely as a humble instrument in the hands of Divine Providence, for the accomplishment of a great end—as the lowly individual, to whose lot it had fallen to introduce into the world a System of Education, so eminently calculated to promote the best interests of mankind, so intimately connected with the formation of sound principles, good morals, and virtuous habits, and consequently so powerful an auxiliary of true religion and genuine piety. He never arrogated to himself any superiority in literature, science, or philosophy. He would carefully guard against all pretensions to abstruse knowledge, deep research, or any of those attainments, for which men ordinarily most value themselves, or seek to be valued by others.

The humblest talents were sufficient for his purpose, combined with what he does not disclaim — a portion of enthusiasm, indefatigable industry, and inflexible perseverance. His researches have not gone beyond a practical study of the infant mind. His aim has been to enter, as it were, into the heart, and to explore the affections, passions, and genius of childhood, so as to apply them to the ends to which they appear to have been fitted, by INFINITE WISDOM,—for promoting the *comfort, happiness, and improvement of early life.* With this object perpetually in view, " I tried (says the Author, in his original Preface to the Report of the Madras Asylum, bearing date 1796, and published in London 1797) every method which a *long and earnest attention to the nature and disposition of youth* suggested, to accomplish these ends to my own satisfaction." p. 5. *

These trials, after various success, terminated in a discovery, which he can only impute to a felicitous concurrence of circumstances — to the charge which he had taken upon himself—to the necessity imposed upon him, by the want of competent assistants—and to the uniform support which he experienced, in all his doings, from the Government

* When a page is quoted without any addition, the reference is to the *original Report* of the Madras Asylum, reprinted, *verbatim et literatim*, 1812 and 1813, and still in print.

under which, and from his Colleagues (the Directors) with whom, he acted.

Whatever has been done subsequently to this discovery, has flowed from the fountain-head, at Madras, as water does from its source. Nothing, which relates to its results, has fallen out unfore-seen—nothing unexpected; except that the current of events have outrun his presentiments, and the calculation of his life. When the Madras Asylum was the only school on this system, the Author was wont to say, " You will mark me for an enthusiast; but if you and I live a thousand years, we shall see this System of Education spread over the world." Little did he then imagine that he should have lived to witness the progress already made towards the event to which he looked forward.

In following up his pursuits, the Author must decline, as he has ever done, entering into any controversy with those who have made, or shall make, claims for their country, for themselves, or for others, to the discovery of the Principle of Mutual Instruction, or to improvements in the System of Tuition built upon it. His sole concern is, to uphold the Archetype of this System, as substantiated, recorded, and promulgated in India, and published in London 1797, before any pretensions had been made, or could have been made, to a discovery, which, till then, was not in existence. Whatever is not expressed or implied in the publication alluded to, or does not flow immediately from it, the Author might, without any sacrifice, surrender to any claimant.

In the year 1797, there was no other school, in any part of the world, conducted through the agency of its pupils themselves. Nor was there any publication, in which the principle of Mutual Tuition was even alluded to, or hinted at, as a UNI-VERSAL ORGAN for economising-time, money, and punishment. Language furnished no name for it. In the course of the year before mentioned, the Report, of the Madras Asylum was published in London. Now mark the issue. Schools on its model forthwith sprung up, both in town and country; whence, as soon as the continent and nations were opened by peace for their reception, they have diffused themselves, abroad as well as at home; and, as already stated, have, in the course of the present century, been disseminated over the face of the earth.

The benefits, offered by this system, have been eagerly embraced by persons of all religious persuasions and political sentiments. Under different circumstances, it has accordingly been distinguished by various names, expressive of its origin, its nature, or its object. On its first discovery, at Madras, it was styled the *New System*,—a name by which it is still pretty generally known; and since, not infrequently, the *Madras System*, from the place of its origin. From the National Society, it obtained the appellation of the *National System*. How it came to be denominated *Lancasterian*, and afterwards the *British and Foreign System*, will appear in the sequel. It has also been entitled *Self-Tuition*, because, by it, the school teaches itself; and *Mutual Instruction,* because the scholars instruct one another. It may still more properly be designated *Mutual Discipline;* a term which—taking *discipline* in its original and classical sense, as denoting education, or instruction, and in its secondary and popular meaning, as denoting government and regulation—comprises, in itself, a concise definition of this system, which, by the same means, conducts simultaneously the instruction and order of a school.

Subsequently to the promulgation and exhibition of the Madras System, it has been remarked, that various instances of the partial employment, of scholars in the instruction of one another had been frequently noticed. But these were solitary, unconnected instances; not deduced from any common principle, nor productive of any general results. No attempt had ever been made to copy after them, nor to make them the basis of any theory, or even practical plan. In like manner, one of the most striking *approximations to Mutual Instruction, which* have been industriously brought forward, terminated in the school wherein it began; nor did all the *ingenuity* of an *ingenious people* discover how it could be turned to any useful account. It was not till after the Madras System had been transplanted from England, and exemplified in *their* Metropolis, that the principle of *Mutual Instruction* was appreciated and acknowledged by them as a GENERAL ORGAN for the administration of elementary schools: *then* indeed they applied it accordingly, and gave to it that very *appropriate name.*

Those who have confounded writing on sand, with the Madras System, have imagined that it had long prevailed in India; but the fact is, that Mutual Tuition, in that country, as well in schools for the Natives as for Europeans, owes its origin to the Madras Report, and has been, for the most part, transferred thither by Missionaries and Preceptors trained in the Madras Schools at home.*

After all, it is deserving of particular notice, that the ancient custom of employing Monitors in this country for occasional purposes of instruction and discipline, affords an evident, though partial specimen, however generally overlooked and neglected, of Mutual Tuition. But their use was restricted to particular offices, for the relief and assistance of the Master in his labours, seemingly without any view to enlarge the number of his scholars, or to supersede adult Ushers. Instances of this practice were heretofore noticed only as individual facts. No suggestion arose out of them to try its efficacy, in every department of the school, and to ascertain the extent to which it could be carried with advantage. No *experiment* was instituted to deduce, by the Baconian induction of particulars, a set of general rules and laws, and thence to arrive at a universal principle, grounded on facts and observation.

THIS EXPERIMENT was reserved for the Madras Asylum†, and was there made with complete suc-

* See Bengal and Bombay Reports, and Reports of National Society.

† See Experiment made at Madras, passim 1789—1796.

cess. The conclusion arrived at, and confirmed by the experience of every succeeding year, is so *simple* and *plain*, that, however great the advantages produced by its effects may be, they can reflect little, if any, share of credit on the Author. The conclusion arrived at was merely this: that *children, under the instruction, guidance, superintendence, and assistance,* whenever necessary, *of the master* can, and do, teach one another, not only as well as, but far better than, adult ushers, and even than the master himself.

But be this as it may, it is evident that it can in no wise detract from the praise due to the great and good men who have heretofore laboured in the vineyard of Education, that they did not conduct their schools on this *principle,* any more than blame could be imputed to the mariner of old, who did not steer his vessel by the magnetic needle, or propel it by the steam engine, before the application of these instruments to nautical purposes. The words of an able divine and scholar, in speaking of the founders of our old Charity Schools, apply with peculiar propriety, at this time, to the preceptors of great schools over the world. Comparing the humblest discovery, of any moment, with the grandest and most sublime ever made, he says, " If we do not reproach the philosophers of old times with the ignorance of what a Newton saw and investigated, we must not find fault with those good men for not having forestalled the merits, and anticipated the discoveries, of a Bell."*

---

* Sermon preached before the Society for promoting Christian

The examples, however, of the successful employment of monitors of old, are so many experiments made, and facts established, in support of the principle of Mutual Tuition, which will not weigh the less, that there was no view at the time to deduce this inference from them. Formerly, Mutual Tuition was secondary, incidental, partial, and limited; now it is primary, inherent, universal, and all but exclusive. " The point has been gained upon which the judicious instructor may take his stand, and direct the mind in whatever it pleaseth him."*

On the whole, no system, either in theory or practice, having arisen out of any former partial and detached examples, the *principle* was not discovered; while, on the contrary, it may, with equal truth, be asserted, as the subsequent history will shew, by the *clearest and most incontrovertible evidence*, that *every one* of the almost innumerable schools now every where existing, which are conducted through the agency of the scholars, can, without exception, be traced, either directly or indirectly, to the fountain-head at Madras.

Such are the grounds on which the Author presumes to address himself to those who are not yet fully alive to the real spirit and tendency of this System, nor aware of the ultimate objects which it has in contemplation—objects which, there can be

---

Knowledge, at the Anniversary Meeting of the Charity Schools, at St. Paul's, by the very Rev. C. Bethell, D. D. Dean of Chichester. 1817.

* See p. 51 infra.

no hesitation in saying, are as grand and momentous, as the means employed for their attainment
are simple and lowly. This is, in truth, a debt which
the Author considers. himself to have contracted
with society, by the discovery he originally made
and promulgated; by the pledges he has given in
his successive publications, and by the labours and
sacrifices of the best part of a long life, devoted to
this pursuit.

There is but one way in which he conceives he
can acquit himself of this obligation; and that is,
by a steady perseverance in maintaining and per-
petuating, in its primitive simplicity and purity,
a *System of Education*, endowed with such quali-
ties, directed to such ends, and productive of such
results. He accordingly feels it his bounden duty,
in preparing and giving to the world a new edition
of a Manual of the Madras System of Education,
to endeavour to compress, within the narrowest
compass, a distinct view of its essential principle, a
well authenticated narrative of its origin and progress, and a simple, clear, and economical code of
instruction, for its execution, in all its details.

Such a Treatise, if he could do justice to the
facts of the case, and to his conception of the
subject, would go far to dispel the delusion, which
long prevailed, and, in no small degree, still pre-
vails, as to the genuine character of this System,
to vindicate it from the misconstructions and
misrepresentations which have been put upon it,
and to rescue it from that quackery, by which
it has been debased, and from all interpolations

at variance with the spirit of the New School, and repugnant to the genius of children, which, of course, have a direct tendency to bring it into discredit, impair its usefulness, derange, and so far impede its movements. Its progress they cannot arrest; no force can withstand an inherent power, which is indestructible, interminable, and irresistible.

In such a Manual, the reader will likewise be furnished with a touchstone, which will enable him to bring to the test every projected or pretended improvement of the System ; the practitioner will be put in possession of an experienced and faithful guide to conduct him in the path, which has been successfully trodden for upwards of a quarter of a century: and, by the distribution of this volume abroad, as well as at home, it may, perhaps, serve not only to correct present mistakes and errors, but hand down to posterity, in every quarter of the globe, a faithful and authentic Report of the Madras System of Education in its principle, its object, its machinery, its bearings, and its necessary consequences.

But that the Reader, who may not have leisure, or inclination, to enter into details, or to peruse the following History and Manual, may form an idea of the constitution of the Madras School; it is thought advisable to introduce here, a brief exposition of its characteristic principle, and subordinate practices.

§ II. *On the Organ or distinctive Principle of the Madras System.*

"Philosophia, vero omnium mater artiam, quid est aliud, nisi ut Plato ait donum (ut ego inventum) deorum?"—CIC. *Tusc. quæst.* Lib. I.

The Madras System of Education, as before stated, has its seat in the infant mind. It bears no resemblance to those idle and unprofitable speculations of fanciful writers, which have no foundation in the nature and genius of children, or in any well grounded knowledge in the science, or even experience, in the art, of tuition—theories which have not been reduced, and are not, perhaps, reducible, to practice. It is, on the contrary, entirely practical, and grounded on experiments. Neither does it resemble any of the modern systems, which are solely known by the *names* of the masters, who practise them, while *no one can tell* in what they consist. It, on the other hand, admits of a brief definition, and was, from the beginning, defined accordingly, to be " *a new mode of conducting a school, through the medium of the scholars themselves.*" p. 24.

It is the result of a discovery made within the walls of a school, and there carried into complete effect, and to an extent, beyond which, as to its principle, it is impossible ever to carry it. No school can, in this respect, do more than was accomplished in the Parent School at Madras. There the School " *was entirely taught by the boys.*" p. 48.

There is a faculty, inherent in the human mind, of conveying and receiving Mutual Instruction. Like polarity in the magnet, after its attractive

properties were known, this faculty, though partially and occasionally employed in the case of
monitors, had lain hidden for ages in the human
breast, as to any general, and greatly beneficial
purposes. It is this faculty, or rather the development, exercise, and application of this
faculty, that constitutes the Madras System—
the *organ* desiderated by Lord Bacon, for the
multiplication of power, and division of labour, in
the moral and intellectual world—for the communication, extension, and advancement of letters,
arts, and sciences, in general; though it has been
applied, in the first instance, to the science of
education, and the art of tuition—an *organ*, not
the work or invention of man, but " Donum Dei,"
" *the gift of God*," which, like the principle of
gravitation in the material world, pervades, actuates, invigorates, and sustains the entire scholastic system.

Founded on an innate faculty of the human
mind, a principle simple and immutable in its
nature, powerful in operation, and universal in
application, this system will last as long as man
remains constituted as he is at present—as long
as the power of interchanging thoughts, by speech,
writing, and printing, shall endure; nor will its
extension be limited by any other bounds than
those of the habitable globe.

On this principle, a superior can conduct any
institution, how numerous soever, through the
instrumentality of its own members. In a school,
it gives to the master *the hundred eyes of Argus,
the hundred hands of Briareus, and the wings of*

Mercury. By multiplying his ministers at pleasure, it gives to him indefinite powers; in other
words, it enables him to instruct as many pupils as
his school-room will contain.

Here, then, lies the essential distinction between
the *New School,* by which term I designate every
school conducted on the principle of Mutual Instruction, of whatever description or denomination;
and the *Old School,* under which appellation I
include every school anterior to the discovery
made at Madras, and every school posterior to
it, which has not availed itself of that discovery.

It need scarcely be remarked, that Mutual
Instruction implies the requisite arrangement of
its pupils into classes, as in the Old School; but
the law, by which this arrangement is regulated,
and which enables every scholar to determine and
ascertain for himself his appropriate place, renders
the classification in a great measure new, and
gives entire scope to another principle, also inherent in the human breast—*that* of a *virtuous
and generous emulation, which* is peculiarly predominant in the unsophisticated and uncorrupt
mind of youth; *which* is a chief auxiliary in the
New School; and *which,* with the perpetual presence and vigilance of the teachers, supersedes
the necessity of corporeal infliction, or chastisement.

Such is the constitution of the New School.
Its classes—formed on a law, according to which
every pupil finds his level—are entirely conducted
by teachers, selected from among the scholars

themselves, under the superintendence, guidance, and direction of the master.

§ III. *On the subordinate Practices of the New School.*

In detailing and discussing the various arrangements and processes, which have been adopted in the New School, the Author would carefully guard against the possibility of their being identified or confounded with the principle on which the System is built, or the Organ by which it is carried into effect. These are as distinct as discovery and invention, in the proper sense of the terms. The new Organ is, as we have seen, a discovery " *sui generis*"—" *Divinæ particula auræ;*" the work of nature, not of art—one, simple, immutable, and universal. The practices, or subsidiary arrangements and methods, adapted to the development of the energies of this Organ, are of a description quite different. They are inventions in contra-distinction to discovery;—the contrivances of man, optional, arbitrary, limited, and applicable solely to particular branches of instruction and discipline;—contrivances which may be multiplied and diversified at pleasure, and even set aside, without essentially affecting the character of the System, which is quite independent of them, and which communicates its immense powers to all sorts of scholastic processes, that may be substituted in their stead, or are applicable to the instruction of the youthful mind.

When, therefore, the Author inculcates, with earnestness, the advantage of certain subordinate

contrivances, he must be understood to speak of
them merely as compared with other practices of
a similar description; for none of them admit of
comparison with the main spring of Mutual Instruction, which is the vital spirit of the whole;

"———— totamque infusa per artus
Mens agitat Molem, et magno se corpore miscet."

At the same time, he would not willingly forego
the benefit of his long experience, as to the
minor practices and arrangements for conducting
the operations of the New School.

Previously to the discovery of the principle of
Mutual Instruction in the Madras Asylum, and
to the consequent arrangements for the administration of the school, by means of the new
Organ, several modifications, and novel processes,
in the art of tuition, as it then existed, had been
introduced by the Author. These were of course
ingrafted on the New System. One of them, and
one only, was borrowed from an Indian School, as
was stated at the time, in these words: " I had, at
first sight of a Malabar school, adopted the idea
of teaching the letters in sand spread over a board
or bench before the scholars, as on the ground in
the schools of the natives of this country." p. 24.
Other novel modes were spelling on and off book,
syllabic reading, unreiterated spelling, registers,
juries, and many more, of which it is said, in the
Report, " So much for the first minutiæ, which I
have detailed as a specimen. Were I to pursue
this subject through all its stages I should fill a
volume." p. 28.

A series of books, adapted to the New Schools,

was left to be prepared at home; and the process of time, and the ingenuity of the age, have
presented the facilities derived from stereotype
printing and the lithographic press.   But the common source of all these, except the economy of the
recent inventions in printing, is the original record
of the Parent School.

All of them consist in simplifying and carrying
to their just length, the primary methods of that
school, and in discarding all unprofitable lessons,
such as idle stories, and tables of unmeaning and
unconnected monosyllables and polysyllables, &c.
No task is ever given, which does not exercise
the faculties, cultivate the understanding, improve
the memory, and add to the stock of useful knowledge.   In the very beginning, the scholar learns
the alphabet, to write, to spell, and to read in
one act, and exercises his little mind (which delights him) in dictating a series of lessons under the
head of each letter, as he copies it in order, by
which he unites every consonant with every vowel,
and every vowel with every consonant.

He then enters on a course of moral and religious, useful and amusing instruction, in which
every copy in writing is a lesson in spelling and
reading, and *vice versâ*, while, at the same time,
the members of the class examine one another on
the meaning of every word and sentence.

On the first day of his admission into school, the
child begins the study of arithmetic, by a quarter
of an hour's lesson, once or twice a day, according to circumstances, which forms a relaxation from
other studies, and an agreeable change to the mind.

While, in the common way, the pupil is solely employed in learning to write the idle digits, the intellect being locked up all the time, a child instructed in a Madras School, in the act of copying the digits, goes through an elementary course of the four cardinal rules, constituting, in reality, the whole of arithmetic, in a series of successive lessons,—all of which, after a little instruction, he dictates for himself, must consequently understand, and cannot forget.

To sum up the whole: The Madras System consists in conducting a school, by a single Master, THROUGH THE MEDIUM OF THE SCHOLARS THEMSELVES, by an uniform and almost insensibly progressive course of study, whereby the mind of the child is often exercised in anticipating and dictating for himself his successive lessons, by which the memory is improved, the understanding cultivated, and knowledge uniformly increased— a course in which reading and writing are carried on in the same act, with a law of classification, by which every scholar finds his level, is happily, busily, and profitably employed every moment, is necessarily made perfectly acquainted with every lesson as he goes along, and without the use or the need of corporeal infliction, acquires habits of method, order, and good conduct, and is advanced in his learning, according to the full measure of his capacity.

§ IV. The Author cannot yet prevail with himself to dismiss this prospectus, without still further transgressing the bounds which he had originally set to this Introduction. He cannot forbear adding one word more, in this place, to the Institutors and Preceptors of Village Schools, and with an *earnest and anxious entreaty to* PARENTS to observe; that it is a common (and to many a child a grievous and fatal) error to imagine, that the Madras System is of no use but in large schools. On the contrary, the methodical and systematic course of study, and the subordinate practices* in the New School, are as applicable to a single child in a family, as to a numerous class in a school. It is true, indeed, that the economy of this System depends upon the number of scholars, as well as upon the superior despatch in teaching, and that the important advantages of imitation and emulation have full scope only where there is a competent number of classes, of a competent size. But even the grand principle of Mutual Instruction applies, in some measure, to a school, however small. If there are only two children in the same stage of the course, by appointing the one tutor to the other, they will derive double pleasure and double benefit. This advantage grows with the number of scholars. Six scholars form a respectable class, though thirty-six is much better.

§ V. It may be here also noticed, (for still the

---

* Such as writing on sand and slate, learning alphabetical and monosyllabic lessons in a series, with which the child can proceed of his own accord, syllabic reading, unreiterated spelling, simultaneous reading and writing, reading by pauses, and the course of arithmetic, which the child, as soon as initiated by two or three examples, can dictate for himself.

Author cannot refrain himself from one more remark due to his subject,) that in order to instruct the whole of the poor population, the number of children, at one time, in parochial and district schools, if educated on the New System, will be far less than has hitherto been calculated on the Old System, even if instruction be carried much farther; for it will be finished in a space of time far, very far, less than can be well imagined by those who witness the slovenly, defective, and imperfect manner in which Mutual Instruction is usually conducted, even in many respectable schools. Hence a wide field will be opened for *industry, the appropriate virtue of the poor:* but of this in another place.

The courteous Reader who will advance one step further, and peruse the ensuing sketch of the history of the Madras School, will find *decisive and conclusive proofs* in confirmation and corroboration of the facts which have been adduced, the statements which have been made, and the positions which have been laid down, in this Prospectus.

To conclude, as was begun, in words of high authority:

" There are several ways of reforming men, by the laws of the civil magistrate, and by the public preaching of ministers. But the most likely and hopeful reformation of the world must begin with children. Wholesome laws and good Sermons are but slow and late ways; the timely and the most compendious way is a good education. This may be an effectual prevention of evil, whereas all afterways are but remedies, which do always suppose some neglect and omission of timely care."—TILLOTSON.

PART I.

SKETCH OF
DISCOVERY, PROMULGATION, AND DIFFUSION
OF THE
New or Madras System.

CHAP. I. *On the Discovery of " A System of Tuition altogether New."* [*]

THE NEW OR MADRAS SYSTEM OF EDUCATION *originated* in the MILITARY MALE ORPHAN ASYLUM, at Egmore, near Fort St. George, in the East Indies. This Institution was founded, by orders of the Court of Directors, about the same time, and for a similar purpose, with the ROYAL MILITARY ASYLUM AT CHELSEA, " for the EDUCATION and MAINTENANCE of the *Orphan and Indigent Sons* of the European Officers and Soldiers of the Madras Army." One moiety of the expense was borne by the Company, as far as one hundred scholars; the other was defrayed by voluntary contribution. The subscribers, in a few years, doubled the original complement, and have since extended the numbers as occasion required.

Sons of European officers, and others in affluence, were admitted as boarders to the same fare and treatment as the boys on the foundation—an arrangement, which, while it added to the numbers, improved the funds of the school. These supernumerary pupils do not properly fall within the object of this Narrative, otherwise than as partaking of the common benefits of the establishment.

Of this Institution, the Governor of Fort St. George was President: the Commander-in-Chief, and other Members of Council, Vice-Presidents: the Chaplains, and principal civil and military servants of the Company, Directors: and the Church-wardens of St. Mary's, Treasurers. The Author, a minister of that church, a chaplain of Fort St. George, a Director of the Asylum, a subscriber to the establishment, and much attached to the army, undertook the superintendence, on the

---

[*] Circular Letter of the Government of Madras. *Infra*, p. 27.

B

stipulation, that the salary, annexed to the office, should be added to the revenues of the school, till a professional and more competent superintendent could be found. For reasons, which will appear in the sequel, he continued in that charge, till the declining state of his health would not admit of his remaining any longer in India.

In the year 1789, the school was opened, and, before the expiration of that year, the Author entered on his office. In the earnest and anxious discharge of his functions, he conceived the design of rescuing a race of children from the state of degradation into which they were sunk, by a vicious education, and in which they were retained by public opinion.* With this view, he proposed to himself to form the school on the best models then known, and to give to the education of its pupils, a direction suited to their condition, and to the wants of the community.

This undertaking was attended with peculiar difficulties, not only from the habits of the half-caste children, who were the most numerous objects of the charity, but also from the want of co-operation on the part of the masters, some of whom did not possess the qualifications requisite for the accomplishment of the object, which he had at heart; nor could they, in that country, be replaced by others better qualified. He did not, however, relax his exertions, or despair of ultimate success. The discouragements, which he met with, served only to stimulate the workings of a mind perpetually intent on its object.

---

* " The school promises fair to present to me the sole reward I have sought, of all my labours with my young pupils, by giving to society an annual crop of good and useful subjects, many of them rescued from the lowest state of depravity and wretchedness. If the spirit I have tried to infuse into the minds of our youth do not evaporate, I despair not of proving, to the observant spectator, that it is the perversion of every right principle of education, which has hitherto, more than any other cause, stamped the characters of the half-caste children. Suppose, only, deceit and trick, taught by the parent, who has generally the charge of the infant mind, as well by example as by precept, and you will readily imagine the consequence. To correct this radical error will ever be the most difficult part of my task; and it is therefore I have bent my utmost endeavours to root out this perversity."—*Extract of Letter to G. Dempster, Esq. of Dunichen, M. P.* 15th June, 1794.

After various trials*, with various success, to improve the state of the school, he had recourse, on a particular emergency, to an expedient, the success of which opened to him fresh prospects, gave a new bent to his efforts, and, by rendering him independent of all but his pupils themselves, in advancing their profit and happiness, carried his ideas far beyond his original purpose. It was simply this :—

One of the masters, as they were styled, the usher of the lowest class in the school, having, after repeated trials and frequent admonitions, failed in the performance of a task assigned to him, excused himself on the usual plea, offered by ignorance, indolence, and indifference, that " *it was impossible.*"

The Author, though not diverted from his purpose, was made sensible that he must be defeated in his schemes, if he depended, for their execution, on the will or ability of those under him, whose minds he could not command. In this dilemma, he bethought himself of committing the charge of the class to one of the boys of the school, on whose obedience, disposition, and talents, he could confidently rely. What the master had pronounced impossible, this boy (by name, JOHN FRISKIN), who had learned the elements of his letters (his A, B, C,) at the Asylum, executed at once, and with ease. He was, of course, appointed permanent teacher of the class. The success exceeded expectation. This class, which had been before worse, was now better taught, than any other in the school.

The experiment which, from necessity, had been tried with one class, was now, from choice, gradually extended to every other, in progression, from the lowest to the highest. The success was uniform, the discovery was complete. The masters, as far as regarded the instruction of the school, were entirely superseded. The school " *was entirely taught by the boys,*"—a foundation, never to be shaken, was laid, of a new and efficient system of education. The history of this discovery is thus briefly told in the official Report of the School :

---

* See Preface to Madras Report.

" I soon found that, if ever the school was to be brought into good order, and taught according to that method and system, which is essential to every public institution, it must be done, either by *instructing ushers in the economy of such a seminary, or by youths from among the pupils, trained for the purpose.* For a long time I kept both of these objects in view; but was in the end compelled, after the most painful efforts of perseverance, *to abandon entirely the former, and adhere solely to the latter.* I found it difficult, beyond measure, to new model the minds of men of full years; and that whenever an usher was instructed so far as to qualify him for discharging the office of a teacher of this school, I had formed a man who could earn a much higher salary than was allowed at this charity, and on far easier terms. My success, on the other hand, in training my young pupils in habits of strict discipline and prompt obedience, exceeded my expectation; and every step of my progress has confirmed and riveted in my mind the superiority of THIS NEW MODE OF CONDUCTING A SCHOOL THROUGH THE MEDIUM OF THE SCHOLARS THEMSELVES." p. 22.

Such was the complete establishment of " *a system of tuition altogether new,*" " by which a school or family *may teach itself,* under the superintendence of the master or parent." Nothing remained to be done — nothing more has been done — and nothing more can be done, as far as regards the GENERAL PRINCIPLE which constitutes the Madras System of Education. No school can do more than TEACH ITSELF through the agency of its scholars. In a word, the following diagram gives a body and shape to this system, which, if all other monuments of it should perish, would alone serve as a sufficient memorial to revive and perpetuate it. Here it is seen that the Madras Asylum was entirely taught by boys from seven to fourteen years of age; and the classification, employed in the execution of the arrangement for this purpose, is also rendered obvious to sense. It is a literal copy of the scheme of the School, from the official Report, to which, as the archetype of the New System, a perpetual reference will be made.

It may be proper to observe, that, in consequence of a late addition to the former complement of the School, many of the boys, of the lower classes, had been recently admitted.

LIST of Boys on the Foundation of the Charity who are Teachers in the Male Asylum, &c.

Class.	Teacher.	Age (Yrs. Mos.)		Time in School (Yrs. Mos.)		Assistants.	Age (Yrs. Mos.)		Time in School	No. of Boys in each Class.	Total.	DAILY TASKS.
1	C. Hancock	14	16	7		T. Adamson	11	114	6	34		Enfield's Speaker, Bible, Spectator, Writing, Arithmetic vulgar and decimal, Book-keeping, Grammar, Geography, Geometry, Mensuration, Navigation, and Astronomy*.
2	G. Stevens	14	37	4						25		Enfield's Speaker, Bible, Spectator, Writing, Arithmetic, and Grammar.
3	W. Faulkner	12	87	2						25		Enfield's Speaker, Testament, Spectator, Writing, Arithmetic, and Grammar.
4	R. Kentish	11	63	7		R. Steele	7	91	6 9	11	95	Select Stories, Writing, Arithmetic, and Tables.
						T. Jones	9	75	5 10			
						J. Gore	9	28	2 16			
						T. H. Morris	8	98	8 17			
5						J. Shaw	11	34	4 12	19		Testament, Writing, and Tables.
6	J. Friskin					W. Lantwar	11	66	3 9	9		Spectator, Writing, and Arithmetic.
7	has charge					W. Anchant	9	85	8 9	9		Psalter, Writing, and Catechism.
8	of the rest	12	87			F. Lawrence	9	05	10 9	9		Spelling-book, Writing, and Catechism.
9	of the											Child's Second Book, Stops, Marks, and Hymns.
10	school as											Child's First Book, and Figures.
11	follows.											Monosyllables.
12												Great and small Alphabet.

Under the charge of John Friskin Teachers . . . . 14 / 91

Total 24th June, 1796 200

* In regard to several of these sciences, nothing more is meant, in general, than that some of the boys, for whom it may seem eligible, are initiated in their first elements; so that if their future destination, or profession, or situation, require it, they may hereafter be able to build on the foundation which has been here laid.

CHAP. II.   *On the Promulgation of the New System of Education in India.*

THE facts which have been stated in the foregoing chapter do not, as has been said, rest on *personal averment,* or on anonymous testimony: they stand on official and public records and vouchers, attested by the highest authorities in India.   If the discovery, of which the rise has been related, had not been committed to writing, or if it had been locked up within the walls of the school in which it was made, or in the books of the Asylum in which it was recorded, the new system of tuition might have gradually fallen into decay, and grown into desuetude; and the discovery itself might, in the course of time, have been lost to the world.   To prevent this— no unusual occurrence — was the uniform study of the Author.   On his first experience of the manifest improvement in the conduct, progress, and happiness of his pupils, he adopted the resolution of drawing up, for the general meetings, annual Reports of the measures, the results of which had gone *"far beyond the most sanguine hopes."* p. 58.   These Reports were regularly entered on the records of the Asylum, and transmitted by the Government of Fort St. George to the Court of Directors at home.

After seven years, devoted to the completion of the work which he had undertaken, and when he was now enjoying the fruits of his labours, he was under the painful necessity of relinquishing his interesting charge, and returning to Europe for the recovery of his health. On the first intimation of his intention, he was officially called upon to digest a compendium of the annual Reports, with a summary of his new method of instruction and discipline, as at that time matured and established, for the guidance of his colleagues, in the direction of the Institution, and also for a model to his successors in the superintendence of the School, that *the new system* might be perpetuated in a situation, where it had been attended with such signal success.

His final Report, drawn up on this occasion, and bearing date the 28th of June, 1796, was entered, by order of a General Meeting of the President, Vice

Presidents, and Directors, on the records of the Asylum, and transmitted, by the Government of Fort St. George, not only, like the former Reports, to the Court of Directors at home, but also to the Governments of Calcutta and Bombay. The circular, which accompanied and authenticated this last Report, as well as the whole tenor of the Report itself, bears indisputable testimony, that the Government of Madras, as well as the author, had their eyes fixed upon, and actually anticipated, not only the particular, but also the general, diffusion of the discovery made in the Institution under their patronage, and of the system of education grounded on that discovery.

The following copy of this document, which was sent to the supreme Government, will speak for itself:—

To THE HONOURABLE SIR JOHN SHORE, BART., GOVERNOR GENERAL IN COUNCIL, AT FORT WILLIAM.

Honourable Sir, *Dated 6th August*, 1796.

The Military Male Orphan Asylum having flourished under "*a system of tuition altogether new*," we are desirous of diffusing, especially in India, the Report of its progress, and present state, and the *mode of teaching* practised there, with a view to *extend* any benefits, which may arise from this system, amongst that class of children to whom it seems peculiarly adapted.

We have, therefore, the honour of transmitting a copy of the Rev. Dr. Bell's *last Report of the School, extracted from the Records of the Institution,* which we recommend, as deserving the attention of those who interest themselves in the education and welfare of the rising generation.

We have the honour to be, with respect, Honourable Sir, your most obedient humble Servants,

(*Signed*) HOBART, ALURED CLARKE, EDWARD SAUNDERS, E. W. FALLOFIELD.

Thus ended the history of the Madras System, during the Author's residence and superintendence, in India: And such was the completion of a System of Education, destined to be as permanent as the faculty of the human mind, on which it is founded.

Having thus acquitted himself of his *scholastic task at Madras,* he fondly imagined that, with his official station, must terminate his official labours in the vineyard of

education. On his arrival at home, if, as he conceived
must be the case, without station or authority, he did not
see, how he could, or need, do more, to forward his
ulterior objects, than publish the Madras Report, and
put it into the hands of those in power—of parents, and
of masters of schools, and other seminaries of learning,
with a proffer of his gratuitous services.

CHAP. III. *On the Publication of the Madras System
of Education in London, and its Introduction into
English Schools.*

ON the arrival of the Author at home, 1797, he published, *verbatim et literatim,* the said Report of the
Madras Asylum, as transmitted by the Right Honourable Lord Hobart (late Earl of Buckinghamshire), President in Council at Fort St. George, to the Court of
Directors of the East India Company.

The character and principle of the system, recorded in
that publication, are thus set forth in the title page:—

" *An Experiment in Education, made at the Male Asylum at
Madras; suggesting a System, by which a School or Family may
teach itself, under the Superintendence of the Master or Parent.*"
London, 1797.

The Preface of this experiment is equally explicit as
to the object of the system; which was, " *to make good
men, good subjects, good Christians.*" And it concludes with these words, " That further and similar trials
may be made, and the success, in every instance, ascertained by experience, is the aim of this publication."
To the same effect is the entire drift of the Report itself.

Experiments have accordingly been made, and so far
the results do not belie the expectations which the Author
entertained. Within less than a year, after its promulgation in England, it was introduced under the auspices of
the late D. P. WATTS, ESQ., of *Portland Place,* into
the oldest Protestant Parochial School in the City of
London—St. Botolph's, Aldgate*; and, soon after, the
Schools of Industry at Kendal were organised precisely
on the model of the Madras Asylum, under the patronage
and personal superintendence of the Mayor of that town,

---

* See pp. 51, 52, infra.

Dr. Briggs, an eminent physician, now settled at Liverpool. These schools attracted the early notice of Sir Thomas Bernard, Bart. In September, 1800, he spent several days in a minute inspection of them, and drew up a detailed account of the new method of instruction practised there, which he published in the *Reports of the Society for bettering the Condition of the Poor.* To take no notice of several other schools, in different parts of the kingdom, which, at that time, were partially conducted upon the same model, two extracts from this popular and widely-circulated publication will suffice to prove that the Madras System of Education was well understood, faithfully copied, and ably executed, in this country, before the end of the last century, without any other help or guide than the Report of the Madras Asylum; for, at that time, the Author was not personally known either to Dr. Briggs, or Sir Thomas Bernard.

" During the Master's absence, the care of the School was put under Monitors. The School was as well conducted during that month of the Master's absence, and the progress of the instruction was as great, as at any other time."*

The account closes with these words:—

" But let the reader beware how he ventures hastily to reject all this, as impracticable theory; for it is a plain and literal account of the Male Asylum at Madras, as it existed in 1796, under the superintending care of the Rev. Dr. Bell."*

The aim of the author, as expressed in the Preface of his original publication, as well as in the Report itself, was already, in a great degree, realised. It was ascertained that the success of the Madras experiment did not depend upon accidental or local circumstances—upon any peculiarities in the government or climate of India—or upon the condition and genius of the pupils of the Parent School. At Kendal, as at Egmore, was exhibited a complete model of a school, on a " *System of Tuition altogether new;*" by which the instruction and discipline were entirely conducted by the pupils.

That the system was as well understood in theory, as exemplified in practice, before the conclusion of the last

* For particulars see the third volume, No. 90, of Society for bettering the Condition of the Poor.

century, will undeniably and abundantly appear from an
early critique on this publication, by an anonymous and
unknown writer.

"One such practical experiment (it is said in the first review
of the report of the Madras Asylum) in education, is worth a
thousand ingenious, but fanciful theories, fabricated in the
closet, and often little calculated for any other sphere....... It
was the steady prosecution of this happy idea [this new mode of
conducting a school through the medium of the scholars them-
selves] that enabled the Doctor to surmount all obstacles, and to
establish a system of education, the effects of which are as truly
interesting as the means are novel.

"As to Dr. Bell, when we consider the object he had in view,
the ingenuity and perseverance displayed in accomplishing that
object, his disinterestedness in declining all pecuniary reward, and
the success with which his endeavours have been crowned, we
feel rejoiced in the opportunity of acknowledging his deserts, and
thus anticipating the opinion of all the true friends of mankind.
For while their esteem and applause were bestowed on Howard,
who visited prisons, and Count Rumford, who has reformed
work-houses, a portion of it will not be withholden from him,
who has successfully endeavoured to render these abodes of
guilt and wretchedness less necessary, by the influence of early
tuition, on the minds and manners of the destitute and abandoned orphan." *Anal. Review for January*, 1799.

There was now nothing left for the present century,
but to follow up the experiment, contrived, digested, and
matured abroad, and repeated with complete success at
home; and to give currency and extension to a new and
intellectual engine of Education, admirably calculated
for the formation and cultivation of the infant mind, and
"to give a new character to society at large;" as it had
done to its original pupils, the half-caste children of
India.

CHAP. IV. *On the general Diffusion of the Madras
System in its genuine Simplicity; and with it of the
Gospel of Peace and Salvation; and on its Tendency
to the speedy Fulfilment of the Prophecies.*

THE Author, on the publication of the Report of the
Madras Asylum, with its documents and vouchers, put
this original record into the hands of those in power—of
the leading Members of the Societies for promoting

Christianity—of the Trustees, Governors, and Masters of Schools, and of Parents, and others, who, he thought, were most likely to avail themselves, for public or private good, of an engine, which was peculiarly fitted for the reformation of scholastic instruction and discipline: and did every thing in his power to propagate the New System, except abandon his clerical duties, and commence professional schoolmaster; which, if he had done, it is not improbable that his purpose might have been defeated. At that time, the minds of men were appalled with the horrors of the war which raged; many of the highest authorities had neither leisure nor inclination to bestow on schemes of innovation, of any description; comparatively few were then to be found friendly to the education of the poor; and still fewer would even listen to the proposal of making any alteration in the *economy* of schools for the richer classes of children, and for the higher branches of study.

But when the machinery of the New School came to be exhibited to public view, and its advantages rendered palpable to sense; and as the subject of the education of the people was more and more discussed, the minds of men were more and more opened to the advantages of training the poor in moral and religious principles, in the elements of useful knowledge, and in habits of diligence and industry. The indifference or reluctance before shewn to any propositions for the general diffusion of a plan, which had been, on the first experiment at Madras, attended with an economy of time, money, and punishment, unknown before, and which, in the earliest repetition of that experiment at home, had been crowned with complete success, was gradually disappearing, or less openly avowed; and schools of *Mutual Tuition* multiplied with an accelerating ratio.

A narrative of their progress and beneficial effects, would swell this sketch far beyond its just limits. Even of the numerous parochial schools, charitable, and other establishments, which the Author had the honour of organising, in all the simplicity of the Madras System, two commanding examples must suffice in this place. One, the noblest monument ever erected to the honour of

this or any other country—the Royal Military Asylum,*
at Chelsea, under the illustrious auspices of His Royal
Highness the Commander-in-Chief, its Founder, Father,
and indefatigable Guardian—an establishment the more
interesting to the Author, because with it the Parent
School of this System was coeval and congenial. To
the patronage of His Royal Highness, and its season-
able exhibition at this Institution, much of its subsequent
progress is to be ascribed.

The other, the Barrington School, at Bishop Auckland,
erected, founded, and munificently endowed, by the
Lord Bishop of Durham,† for the education of all the
poor in the neighbourhood—an institution also not a little
interesting, by its timely appropriation to the training of
monitors for the diffusion of the Madras System throughout
the Diocese, and, eventually, over the kingdom and the
world.

After the Author's attendance for several years at the
Royal Military Asylum, and the matured experience of
the "most complete success," and of the beneficial
effects, of the Madras System in this and various institutions throughout the country, Regimental Schools were
established, by the general orders of Goverment, for the
education of the children of soldiers; and the Author was
called upon to prepare a *Manual of Instructions*‡ for
conducting them, and to superintend and direct, at the
Royal Military Asylum, the training of the Sergeant
Schoolmasters, appointed to carry them into effect.
This being accomplished to the satisfaction of His
Royal Highness, the Author was honoured, as on former occasions, with his gracious thanks, and official
testimonials of his consideration and good wishes.

The triumph of the Madras System of Education, thus
complete in the military department, may, at the same
time, be said to have been consummated in the civil department, by the establishment of the NATIONAL
SOCIETY (incorporated by royal charter,) for the
education of the poor on this plan, in the hope of thereby
(in the words of their Report before quoted) "*giving a*

---

† See p. 51, infra.   † See p. 54, infra.   ‡ See p. 53, infra.

new character to society at large.'' The importance
attached to this institution will be manifestly seen in the
" List of the Committee and Officers."

" *Patron,*—HIS MAJESTY the KING.

" *President,*—The ARCHBISHOP of CANTERBURY.

" *Vice-Presidents and Committee,*—The Lord High
Chancellor; the Archbishop of York; the Earls of
Shaftesbury, Hardwicke, and Liverpool; the Bishops of
London, Durham, Winchester, Lichfield and Coventry,
St. Asaph, Bath and Wells, Worcester, Chichester,
Bangor, St. David's, Salisbury, Norwich, Hereford,
Carlisle, Rochester, Ely, Chester, Gloucester, Oxford,
Peterborough, Llandaff, Bristol, Exeter, Sodor and Mann,
Quebec, Calcutta, Nova Scotia; the Lords Kenyon, Gren-
ville, Redesdale, Colchester, Stowell, Radstock; Right
Honourable R. Ryder; Right Honourable Sir J. Nicholl;
Honourable Mr. Justice Park; Sir J. Langham, Bart.;
Archdeacons Pott, Cambridge, and Watson; Reverend
G. D'Oyley, H. H. Norris, and R. Lendon; E. W.
Egerton, G. W. Marriott, W. Davis, J. Round, Q.
Harris, and J. Trimmer, Esqrs.

" Joshua Watson, Esq. *Treasurer.*

" Reverend Dr. A. Bell, *Honorary Member.*

" Right Honourable the Master of the Rolls, and the
Lord Chief Baron, *Auditors.*

" The Reverend Dr. Walmsley, *Secretary.*"

The success of the measures uniformly pursued by this
Society, will abundantly appear from a bare enumeration
of the amount of children, who have received, and are
receiving, instruction, in schools in union with it.

In 1816, five years after its formation, the numbers were officially reported to be 100,000. In the following year, 1817, they
amounted to upwards of one-half more, 155,000. In the official
Report of last year, (1821,) it is stated, that " very little less
than" (double the former number, viz.) " 300,000 children, are
now receiving sound religious education in schools either united
to the Society, or formed mainly on its principles."

Add to these, all the scholars trained in private, as
well as public institutions, on this system of mutual instruction, and the total amount can hardly be estimated
at less than half a million—a number, which, if the
children of the poor complete their education on the new,

C

(say only) in half the time as on the old, system, will, ere long, exhaust the population : and, if the instruction were conducted on sound principles, and ably administered, every poor child might enjoy the inestimable blessings of moral and religious education, and a change made in the face of society, similar to that made in the race of children who were the original pupils of this system.

Nor can the time be very far distant, when the richer classes of the community shall participate in the boon, already conferred on their poorer brethren, and enjoy the incalculable benefits of a System of Education, which, reason and experience have evinced, is, in an eminent degree, adapted to our noble and ingenuous youth, in whose unsophisticated breasts, the principles of a virtuous and generous emulation are predominant. This event will accomplish the scheme of the Madras System at home; and the whole community will be raised in due proportion, and all will approximate nearer to God and goodness.

But even this event forms a small portion of the triumph to which this System aspires. When we look around us in the world, we behold its progress not less striking and remarkable abroad than at home. It would be in vain to attempt enumeration. The schools every where raised and rising, on a large scale, are monuments of that discovery, by which one man can conduct the instruction and discipline of as many scholars as his room will contain. One quarter of a century only has elapsed since the publication, in London, of the Madras System of Education, and, in less than half that time, was it transplanted into every quarter of the globe; and it has now, as before remarked, reached the remotest regions of the earth, every where diffusing the blessings of moral, religious, and useful knowledge, and carrying the *means of civilization,* and the *glad tidings of peace and salvation* into the bosoms of the benighted and barbarous nations.

Thus has it pleased God, in the merciful dispensation of his providence, to have opened *boundless fields of operation;* for the cultivation of which, the Author would gladly have lent, as far as practicable, his personal aid, if incessant occupation at home, and authorities, to which he deferred, (not to mention age and infirmities,) had not set bounds to his *foreign visitations.* For which see the Author's *Scholastic Tour** on the Continent; with notices of the Schools of Mutual Instruction at Paris, Geneva, Lousanne, Netherlands, &c.; and of Pere Girard at Friburg,—

> "Holy Franciscan Friar! brother! hail!"

—And also the celebrated schools of Pestalozzi at Yverdun; and of Fellenberg at Hofwyl.

In short, abroad and at home, its excellence consists in the facility, economy, and power;—the animating, engaging, and endearing motives, by which it implants religious principles, useful knowledge, virtue, and industry in the hearts, and the habits, of the rising generation, rich as well as poor, to a degree which had heretofore been thought impracticable. Its supreme excellence is, that if duly cultivated, it presents a fair prospect, after every former measure, which had been tried, may be said to have failed, of fulfilling, in the course of time, the predictions of the prophets, and the sure promises of our Saviour and his apostles—that " *all the kingdoms of the earth shall become the kingdoms of God and of his Christ*"—" *the earth shall be full of the knowledge of the Lord, as the waters cover the sea*"—" *all thy children shall be taught of God,*" &c. &c. &c.

" I really think (says a learned judge), that his (Dr. Bell's) Plan, if rightly conducted, is one of the most stupendous engines that ever has been wielded; since the days of our Saviour and his Apostles, for the advancement of God's true religion upon earth. * * * I am not sure that this is not the commencement, by his means, of that glorious era, when the knowledge of the Lord shall cover the earth, as the waters cover the sea." 1812. *Instructions,* &c. 6th Edit. p. 34.

" There are several ways (says Archbishop Tillotson) of reforming men, by the laws of the civil magistrate, and by the public preaching of ministers. But the most likely and hopeful reformation of the world must begin with children. Wholesome laws and good sermons are but slow and late ways; the timely and the most compendious way is a good Education. This may be an effectual prevention of evil, whereas all after-ways are but remedies, which do always suppose some neglect and omission of timely care."

* Vindication of Children, p. 65—80.

The Bishop of Winchester has happily drawn the conclusion as it regards this country, which merits the most
serious consideration on every other account, as well as
because it points to the correction of a material defect in
the constitution of a great part of the National Schools.

" If the plan of Education recently adopted in this country, be
generally maintained in its TRUE SPIRIT AND EXTENT, and the
children, when transferred from these schools into the various
walks of humble and active life, be afterwards regularly supplied
with suitable books, to foster and confirm that *principle of Religion*
which has been instilled into them, and that *sense and habit of
submission to which they have been accustomed,* we may defy all the
machinations of domestic foes to subvert our constitution, or disturb our internal tranquillity, and all the exertions of foreign
enemies to deprive us of our prosperity and glory as a nation."—
*Extract from Charge of the Right Rev. George Tomline, D.D.
F.R.S. Lord Bishop of Winchester,* 1822.

CHAP. V.— *On the partial Diffusion of the Madras
System, under different appellations, particularly
under the denomination of Lancasterian.*

NOT to interrupt the narrative of the diffusion of this
system in the direct channels from the fountain-head at
Madras, no specific mention has hitherto been made of
the collateral branches, which have emanated from the
parent river. Of these the most considerable is, that
which is generally known, and widely circulated,
under the denomination of Lancasterian. The incidents,
which gave rise to this appellation, form an episode
almost unexampled in the history of discoveries; the
details of which will supersede the necessity of any particular notice of the minor streams, that have diverged
from the same source.

For the space of seven years after the promulgation of
the New System of Education in this country, and the
successful repetition of it in English Schools, its discovery, whatever name or shape it assumed, remained
undisputed. Every speculative and practical writer on
this subject, recognised its origin; and every gratuitous
superintendent, or stipendiary schoolmaster, who adopted
this System, referred for his authority and prototype to the
Report of the Madras Asylum. But, of all those who
availed themselves of this discovery, no one was more

particular and minute in his reference to the original which he copied, or more liberal in his acknowledgments to the Author of the System, than Mr. Lancaster.

In his case, many advantages of time, place, and other circumstances concurred to pave the way for his acting a conspicuous part, on the theatre of the New School. He was himself a schoolmaster by profession, and had a *deep stake* in the issue of his experiment. In 1798, a year after the publication of the Madras Report in London, he first opened school. His words are, " In the year 1798, I opened a school for the instruction of poor children." * * * " I knew of no modes of tuition but those usually in practice." Again, speaking of his first efforts, " During several years I had essayed to introduce a better system of tuition into the school, and every attempt had failed."*

On the other hand, the trials of the Madras System of Education, which, it has been seen, were made at the same time, that is, during the three last years of the last century, had proved successful. One of these, as has been stated, was exhibited in the metropolis; another in a provincial town, and was published in a widely circulated journal; and a striking picture of the Madras Report had been drawn in a popular review.† The consequence was, that Mr. Lancaster followed the precedents and recommendations of the last century; and the fact is, that, in the beginning of the present century (1801), he converted his institution into a free school, and introduced into it the Madras System of Education.‡

Situated in the midst of a poor population—open to the public view of the metropolis—favoured by a society of active and liberal Friends, of which, at that time, he became one—and supported by a generous public, his school soon grew in fame and numbers, and exhibited the Madras System on the large scale for which it is so eminently adapted, and on ground which gave ample scope to his enthusiasm and indefatigable exertions.

The display of the mechanical powers of this engine, obtained the countenance and substantial aid of illustrious

---

* See pp. 39, 40, infra.   † See p. 30, supra.
‡ See pp. 39, 49, 52, infra.

personages. These, and other circumstances, contributed, in no small degree, to the promulgation and diffusion of the System of Mutual Tuition. It is due to this
zealous advocate and successful propagator of the Madras System, to tell his tale in his own words; and in
those of his most strenuous friends, and ablest advocates.

CHAP. VI.— *On the primary Testimony of Mr. Lancaster to the Authenticity and Originality of the
Madras System; and on the identity of the Lancasterian with it.*

BY comparing Mr. Lancaster's earliest accounts of his
school, with the Report of the Madras Asylum, it will be
seen how faithfully he copied the original, not only in its
essential and immutable principle of mutual instruction; but also in most of its subordinate practices, and
unessential points, which admit of indefinite variety. To
establish this fact, we need go no further than the primary
statements of Mr. Lancaster himself, extracted from the
first and second editions (which are verbatim the same)
of "*Improvements in Education, as it respects the Industrious. Classes of the Community: containing, a short
Account of its present state, Hints towards its Improvement, and a detail of some Practical Experiments, conducive to that end. By Joseph Lancaster. 1803.*"
pp. 1—65; and from the Appendix to the latter edition,
pp. 67—80; and from "*Improvements in Education, as
it respects the industrious Classes of the Community;
containing, among other important particulars, an account
of the Institution for the Education of one thousand poor
Children, Borough Road, Southwark; and of the New
System of Education on which it is conducted. By
Joseph Lancaster.* Third edition, with additions, 1805."
Of these editions, the first and second were published
anterior to his having any direct or personal communications with the Author; the third, after he had opened an
epistolary correspondence with the Author, visited him,
and perused his MS. at Swanage; and after the Author
had attended his school in the Borough Road; and presented him with fifty copies of his second publication on
the subject of the Madras System of Education. But the

Author purposely refrains from quoting this publication, because written in England.

The chief, and almost sole point, of any interest in this comparison, respects the NEW ORGAN or essential principle of Mutual Tuition, which pervades, actuates, invigorates, and sustains the entire scholastic machine; and which, with the law of classification attached to it, constitutes the Madras System of Education.

Extracts from the Report of the Madras Asylum, published in London, 1797.

1. *On the New Organ or Essential Principle of Mutual Instruction.*

The title-page runs thus:

"An Experiment in Education, made at the Male Asylum, at Madras ; suggesting a *System, by which a School or Family may teach* ITSELF, under the superintendence of the Master or Parent." London, 1797, p. 1.

The Preface announces the purpose of the Author, in promulgating this System.

"That farther and similar trials may be made, and the success, in every instance, ascertained by experience, is the aim of this publication."

The whole tenour of the Report is to this effect.

"I soon found * * * see p. 20 supra, to THIS NEW MODE OF CONDUCTING A SCHOOL THROUGH THE MEDIUM OF THE SCHOLARS THEMSELVES."

"*None of the masters have made a progress in letters, equal to the boys in the first class. Their duty is not to teach, but to look after the various departments of the institution.*" p. 34.

"After this manner THE SCHOOL TEACHES ITSELF; and, as matters now stand, THE SCHOOLMASTER ALONE IS ESSENTIALLY NECESSARY AT THIS

Extracts from "Improvements in Education, &c. By Joseph Lancaster. First, Second, and Third Editions ; 1803 and 1805."

[The pages referred to below, when not otherwise mentioned, are those of the First and Second Editions.]

1. *On the opening of Mr. Lancaster's school, and his early testimony to the origin of the System of mutual tuition.*

"The Institution, which a benevolent Providence has been pleased to make me the happy instrument of bringing into usefuless, was begun in the year 1798. The intention was, to afford children of mechanics, &c. instruction in reading, writing, and arithmetic, at about half the usual price." p. 44.

"During several years I had essayed to introduce a better system of tuition into the school, *and every attempt had failed.*" p. 45.

"I ought not to close my account, without acknowledging the obligation I lie under to Dr. Bell, of the Male Asylum at Madras, who so nobly gave up his time and liberal salary, that he might perfect that Institution, which flourished greatly under his fostering care. He published a tract in 1798 [it should be 1797], entitled 'An Experiment on Education, made

SCHOOL. *He has the charge of the daily disbursements and monthly expenses under the treasurer, and is to attend the school, so as to maintain the observance of the Rules.*

" The great advantage of the System is, that you have *a teacher and an assistant for every class.*" p. 40-1.

" Every class is paired off into *teachers (tutors), and scholars (pupils);* so that a boy has always an instructor at his elbow, who is, in the first instance, answerable for his progress; *then the assistant, then the teacher, then the schoolmaster, and last of all the superintendent.*" p. 42.

" *The school has been entirely taught by the boys, from 1st June,* 1795." p. 48.

In a word, the diagram, p. 25, *supra,* exhibits a complete scheme of this System.

· 2. *On the subordinate Practices of the Madras School.*

In subservience to the universal principle, the Madras System furnishes certain individual and subordinate practices or methods in the *art* of tuition, by which, under the agency of the teachers, its pupils are initiated with greater precision, facility, and expedition, into the rudiments of moral, religious, and useful knowledge.

Some of these are, p. 24, " *teaching*" the alphabet, by writing " *the letters*" with the fingers " *in sand, spread over a board or bench, before the scholars, as on the ground in the schools of the natives of this country;*" a practice which, by the bye, will elucidate a passage in holy writ, better than some commentators have done,

at the Male Asylum at Madras ; suggesting a System, whereby a School, or family, may teach itself under the superintendence of the Master or Parent.' From this publication I have adopted several useful *hints.* I beg leave to recommend it to the attentive perusal of the friends of education and of youth. I am persuaded, nothing is more conducive to the promotion of a system than actual experiment. *Dr. Bell had 200 boys, who instructed themselves,* made their own pens, ruled their books, and did all that labour in school, which, among a great number is light; but resting on the shoulders of the well-meaning and honest, though unwise teacher, often proves too much for his health, and embitters, or perhaps costs him his life. I much regret that I was not acquainted with the beauty of his system, till somewhat advanced in my plan ; if I had known it, it would have saved me much trouble, and some retrograde movements. As a confirmation of the goodness of Dr. Bell's plan, I have succeeded with one nearly similar, in a school attended by almost 300 children." pp. 63, 64.

" In the year 1798, I opened a school for the instruction of poor children, in reading, writing, and arithmetic, and the knowledge of the Holy Scriptures ; the children were taught at the low price of four-pence per week. I knew of no modes of tuition, but those usually in practice." Third Edit. p. 1.

" Tuition, in this school, is conducted solely by the senior boys, employed as teachers : the master treating them with peculiar "spelling syllabically, and(p. 27) *reading syllables by themselves, and words by themselves,*" &c.

3. *On Order and Discipline.*

The whole machinery of the New School, as well as the entire scope of the Madras Report, is, in the words of that Report, (p. 39) " not to correct, but to prevent faults," *** " and to preclude the use of punishment."

To these may be added, (p. 31) " *marked books and registers,*" (p. 43), " *black book and jury,* (p. 78), " the monthly Report of the rank they (the scholars) hold in their respective classes."

4. *On the Object, Result, and Economy of this Experiment, and the Proficiency of its Pupils.*

Its *object,* as already stated, is expressed in the Preface, p. 5. " My purpose was to make *good scholars, good men, and good Christians;*" and in the Report, pp. 49, 50, " It is the grand aim of this seminary to instil into these children EVERY PRINCIPLE AND HABIT FITTING FOR GOOD SUBJECTS, GOOD MEN, GOOD CHRISTIANS."

The *result* of the experiment may be briefly stated in the words of the Report itself (p. 32). " The school is thus rendered a *scene of amusement to the scholar,* and a spectacle of delight to the beholder . . . . . the system . . . . calculated *to promote their welfare, to advance their learning, and to preclude punishment,*" (pp. 43, 44). " *For months together, it has not been found necessary to inflict a single punishment.*" And in the words of the resolution of the President, Vice-Presidents, and Directors, 13th January, 1796, p. 58, " This Institution

attention, and not sparing suitable encouragement where merited ; such is their activity and diligence, that no other assistance is necessary at present, or likely to be so in future. J. L. can say with truth, that owing to these advantages, he has no more labour with 250 children than he formerly had with 80, and can do them superior justice in tuition." p. 14, Third Edition.

" The boys' school was instituted as a free school, by Joseph Lancaster, in 1801, and is actually extended to *seven hundred* boys, who are instructed upon a plan entirely new : by means of which, ONE MASTER alone can educate *one thousand boys,* in reading, writing, and arithmetic, as effectually, and with as little trouble, as twenty or thirty have ever been instructed by the usual modes of tuition." p. 23, Third Edition.

" The whole school is arranged into classes; a monitor is appointed to each, who is responsible for the cleanliness, order, and improvement of every boy in it." p. 37, Third Edition.

" To promote emulation, and facilitate learning, the whole school is arranged into classes, and a monitor appointed to each class." p. 40, Third Edition.

" Every boy is placed next to one who can do as well or better, than himself." p. 89, Third Edition.

" The chief duty of the master is to see that the monitors have done their duty." p. 161, Third edition.

These quotations, on the main principle, may be summed up in the words of Mr. Lancaster of a much later date.

has been brought to a *degree of perfection and promising utility, far exceeding what the most sanguine hopes could have suggested* at the time of its establishment."

The *economy* and annual saving of £960 sterling, and of the superintendent's salary, for seven years, £3860, are also stated in the Report, p. 46—49, and 51, 52.

From the particular statements of the *progress* of the respective classes, the highest and lowest examples are here extracted.

" A youth of seventeen years of age, (William Smith) attended the embassy to Tippoo Sultaun, when the hostage Princes were restored, and went through a course of experiments in natural philosophy, in the presence of the Sultaun, by whom he was detained nineteen days, after the embassy had taken leave, to instruct two of his arzbegs, (Lords of the Requests) in the use of an extensive and elegant philosophical and mathematical apparatus, presented to him by the Government of Madras." pp. 34 and 66—74.

" *Friskin,* of twelve years and eight months, *with his assistants,* of seven, eight, nine, and eleven years of age, *has taught* boys of four, five, and six years, to read the Spectator distinctly, and spell every word accurately as they go along, who were only initiated into the mysteries of their A, B, C, eight months before, and have read the child's first and second books twice over, and gone through two spelling books, the Psalter, a great part of the Old Testament, and all the New; and who can make numbers, with

" I now explicitly state what my plan is, as far as I am concerned. It is A SYSTEM *of order,* whereby *a boy of fourteen* [*] *may govern any number of others.* This is combined with new and economical modes of tuition—reading, writing, and arithmetic." —*Letter of Mr. Lancaster to Professor Marsh (Bishop of Peterborough). Morning Post, September* 23, 1811.

2. *On the subordinate practices, which Mr. Lancaster acknowledges to have borrowed from the Madras Report.*

" Dr. Bell was fully sensible of this waste of time in schools, and his method to remedy the evil was crowned with complete success. I have been endeavouring to walk in his footsteps, in the method of teaching about to be detailed.

" The scholars have a desk before them, with ledges on every side, and it is filled with sand to a level with these ledges; every boy is furnished with a sharp pointed wire to write, or more properly to print with. A word is then dictated by the monitor, for instance, ' beer,' and it is immediately sketched in the sand, by every boy with the point of his skewer, and when inspected by the monitor, another word is dictated as before. It possesses all the advantages before described, as attached to spelling on the slate; applies to this with an increase of advantage, as this class of children lose more than two-thirds of time, which is more than those do who can write. It has this difference, that instead of writing it is printing, and, of

---

* See Diagram, supra, p. 25.

their fingers in the sand, to one thousand; and who have learned hymns, stops, and marks, catechism, tables in arithmetic, and to write." pp. 36, 37.

5. *Recommendation of the System to general adoption, and the conclusion of the Report.*

The Report proceeds with recommending the repetition of this experiment, " *in every charity or free-school,*" and " *in the generality of* PUBLIC SCHOOLS AND ACADEMIES.*" It expresses the " pleasing hope, that a rational foundation were laid for forming the characters of children, and implanting in the infant mind such principles, as might, perhaps, continue through life, check the progress of vice and immorality, meliorate the rising generation, and improve the state of Society." p. 53.

It concludes with these words: (pp. 55, 56.)

" *These children are, indeed, now mine by a thousand ties!* I have for them a parental affection, which has grown upon me every year; *for them I have made such sacrifices, as parents have not always occasion to make to their children.* And the nearer the period approaches, when I must, for a while, at least, separate myself from them, the more I feel the pang I shall suffer, in tearing myself from this charge, and the anxious thoughts I shall throw back upon these children, when I shall cease to be THEIR PROTECTOR, THEIR GUIDE, AND THEIR INSTRUCTOR.

" With these sentiments I commend them to Almighty God, and to your fatherly protection and care."

A. BELL, 28th June, 1796.

course, is more connected with reading, than spelling by writing is."—pp. 78, 79. Appendix.

" The figures are taught in the same manner. Sand is a cheap substitute for books any where, but more so in those parts of the country where the soil is sandy, than in London. This method was taken, in the outline, from Dr. Bell, formerly of Madras; but he did not say, in his printed account of that Institution, whether wet or dry sand was used. It for a long time involved our minor classes in much difficulty, having begun with wet sand: we continued it some time. . . . All these difficulties were obviated, by *my hearing from Dr. Bell,* that it was dry sand."—pp. 46, 47. Third Edition.

" In reading they read lines, or sentences, and sometimes paragraphs, in rotation. They are requested to read every word slowly and deliberately, pausing between each. They read long words in the same manner, only by syllables: thus, in reading the word composition, they would not read it at once, but by syllables, thus, com-po-si-tion, making a pause at every syllable. . . . . I am much indebted to Dr. Bell, late of Madras, for the preceding information on the subject. I have reduced it to practice, and find it does honour to its benevolent inventor: to which I have added several valuable improvements, particularly that of the reading and spelling cards." p. 57—59, Third Edition.

" This method of spelling is commonly practised in schools; but for the method of *studying* the spelling lessons, I am indebted to Dr. Bell, believing it

Such is a brief summary of facts recorded in the minutes of the Madras Asylum, and of the views of that government and of the Author, on their promulgation.

———

N. B. In confirmation of this report, if confirmation can be wanted, the reader is referred to " *A Voyage to India*," by the Rev. James Cordiner, (now Minister of St. Paul's Episcopal Chapel, at Aberdeen). The Author, on his arrival in England, had appointed him to the charge of the Madras Asylum ; and it will be seen in that publication, that when he arrived there, in 1798, he found the school in the state in which the Author left it, as described above.

P. 85, " THE TUITION (says he) OF THE SCHOOL was entirely conducted by the boys themselves ; at least, I was the only grown person among them, in the character of a teacher." " The school was regularly divided into classes ; the boys were paired off into tutors and pupils."***

P. 87, " From the perpetual agency of this System, idleness cannot exist. On entering the school, you can discover no individual unemployed, no boy looking vacantly round him ; the whole is a beautiful picture of the most animated industry, and resembles the various machinery of a cloth manufactory, completely executing their different offices, and all set in motion by one active engine."

After an exposition of the main principle, he proceeds to details of the instruments of discipline, the practices, &c., all of which correspond with the practices so often quoted.

was his peculiar invention." p. 60, Third Edition.

Mr. Lancaster closes the Appendix to his Second Edition, with his repeated recommendation of, and reference to, his archetype, in these words :—" I again refer the reader to Dr. Bell's pamphlet, he cannot do better than to procure one, and read it himself, which will save me going more into detail, and afford him greater satisfaction."

———

Thus faithfully and closely has Mr. Lancaster copied and acknowledged the Report of the Madras Asylum. It would be to no purpose to pursue further the points of identity and similitude between the Madras and what is termed the Lancasterian system. Nor would it avail to enter into details of the numerous other inventions, which occur in his Third Edition ; and which alone, at that time, he claimed as his own. Some of these flow directly from the Madras Report, or resemble the *minutiæ*, of which it is there said, " Were I to pursue this subject through all its stages, I should fill a volume ;" some are quite dissimilar, and some indifferent. Of all of them, a bare recital of their names will pourtray their character.

3. *On Order and Discipline.*

As literally as Mr. L. has in general conformed, and explicitly appealed to, the Madras Report, or to the communications of the Author, in all that is essential and material ; so widely, when he has given reins to his own genius for inventions, has he, in various parts of his Third Edition, deviated from his original : as, for example, in his disquisition "On Offences and Punishments." Third Edition, p. 100—106; from which the following extracts are taken:

1. "Wooden log round his (the culprit's) neck, which serves him as a pillory." 2. "It is common to fasten the legs of offenders together with wooden shackles: one or more, according to the offence." 3. "Should not this punishment have the desired effect, the left-hand is tied behind the back, or wooden shackles fastened from elbow to elbow, behind the back." 4. "Sometimes the legs are tied together." 5. "Occasionally boys are put into a sack, or in a basket, suspended to the roof of the school, in the sight of all the pupils, who frequently smile at the *birds in the cage.* This punishment is one of the most terrible that can be inflicted on boys of sense and abilities." 6. "Frequent or old offenders are yoked together, sometimes by a piece of wood that fastens round their necks; and, thus confined, they parade the school, walking backward. . . . . Four or six may be yoked together in this way." 7. Culprit "dressed up with labels describing his offence, with a tin or paper crown on his head. In that manner he walks round the school, two boys preceding him and proclaiming his fault." 8. "Girls and boys washing and tapping one another's faces." 9. "It is also very seldom that a boy deserves both a log and a shackle at the same time."

From this code of punishments, so entirely repugnant and diametrically opposite to the genius and spirit of the New System, even independently of facts and testimonies, as well as of the confessions of Mr. Lancaster, before quoted; it has been made a question, whether or not, when he adopted the mechanism, and followed the practices of the Madras School, he *understood its principle, imbibed its spirit, or felt its prodigious powers,* which is fitted to, and actually has, when duly administered, put an end to the race of dunces, and to those offences, for which corporal punishments are inflicted.

4. *On other Inventions, which, like the code of punishments, occur in Mr. Lancaster's Third Edition, and he there claims as his own.*

The following list is extracted from *The Origin, Nature, and Object of the New System of Education.* Murray, 1811.

"He (Mr. Lancaster) has invented, — 1st, The number on the wall, under which the boys are to be mustered;—2d, The black colour of the sand board;— 3d, The ledge upon which the boys lean their left arms while using their right hand;—his 4th invention is slinging the hat;—his 5th, slinging the slate;—6th, The numbered paper tickets;—7th, The leathern tickets;—8th, The picture badge;—9th, The order of merit;—10th, The use of slates instead of sand;—11th, The ruling machine;—12th, The lessons, in large print, to be hung upon the wall;—13th, The key and the ignorant teacher." p. 189.

The Third Edition closes with a notice of a fourth edition, in these words: "It will be merely a transcript of the present work, J. L. having no more improvements in a fit state for public view at present."

D

Now let the reader say whether Mr. Lancaster's extraordinary success, consequent on his adoption of the Madras System of Mutual Tuition, can be ascribed to these subsequent inventions. Independently of this new organ, no school ever has produced, or ever can produce such results. It is already fully ascertained by experience, that Schools of Mutual Tuition, even when in practice much of its spirit has evaporated and its genius been grossly violated, have succeeded beyond former examples, however short of its genuine and matured fruits.

The Society, established for the purpose of carrying on this branch of the New System of Education, have, several years ago, superseded Mr. Lancaster, and have taken entirely upon themselves the conduct of the Borough Road School, and of the Institutions connected with it, at home and abroad; and have substituted for *his* name, *that* of *British and Foreign School-Society*. Their proceedings, however, do not fall within the province of this history, except as far as they have been, and are, indefatigable agents in propagating, under a new name (British and Foreign), and on an extensive scale, the System of Mutual Tuition, which they had before carried on, under the name of, and in union with, Mr. Lancaster. All that is here necessary, in justice to them and to him, is, to remark, that, in the course of their progress, they have abandoned much of what was most exceptionable in some of the practices, which had been engrafted on the Madras System, as noticed above.

CHAP. VII. — *On Mr. Lancaster's Retractation of his preceding acknowledgments; on his Claim to the Discovery of the System of Mutual Tuition; and on the Testimony of his Friends and Advocates on that head.*

It may not perhaps be surprising to those well acquainted with human nature, if, after all has been seen, they should find that the astounding success, and incalculable results, which attended the indefatigable labours of Mr. Lancaster, have produced a complete oblivion in his memory, and revolution in his sentiments and statements, relative to the origin of a System of Education, to the propagation of which he had so largely contributed. When the system of mutual instruction had been exhibited to public view, and rendered palpable to sense, in numerous large institutions and free-schools, and exemplified in the Royal Military Asylum, at Chelsea; and when its immense importance, in a moral, religious, and political point of view, came to be appreciated; it was then made a party question where this system originated; whether in the Madras Asylum, or in the Borough-Road School. The advocates and partizans of the claim, which

Mr. Lancaster was now induced to make to the discovery of this system, seemed, as well as himself, to overlook the facts which had previously been related, and
the testimony which he himself had borne to these
facts—they seemed to have forgotten that he had not even
opened school, when the Madras system was published
in London; and that he did not adopt it till it had been
practised, both in town and country, reviewed and promulgated in popular works, and till he had himself, in
three several publications, recorded its origin, with peculiar circumstances of acknowledgment to its Author;
repeatedly appealed to the Madras Report for the authority on which he acted, and referred his reader to it,
"which (he says) will save me going more into detail, and
afford him greater satisfaction." p. 44, supra.

Thus, for example, when Mr. Whitbread introduced
into Parliament his intended Bill on " Poor Laws and
Education," and panegyrised the New System of Education, he ascribed its discovery to Mr. Lancaster.
On this occasion, a friend of Mr. Whitbread's, who had
before put the publications and MSS., and other papers
of the Author, on the subject of Education and Poor
Laws, into his (Mr. Whitbread's) hands, replied, in his
place, that " the discovery of the New System of Education was solely and wholly attributable to his near
neighbour, and respected friend, Dr. Bell."

Soon after, the Author had the honour of an interview
with Mr. Whitbread, which had been promised to him,
through their mutual friend, some months before. This
conference terminated, by his (Mr. Whitbread's) de-
claring that he would do the Author justice, and re-
questing him, " as a particular favour done to himself, to
meet Mr. L. at his house in Dover Street."

To this requisition, the Author returned an answer in
writing: but first it is necessary to notice that Mr. Lancaster, seizing the present opportunity, had circulated
hand-bills through London, panegyrising his Patron, and
broadly proclaiming himself the Inventor of the New
System of Education, and had also published the following advertisement:—

" IMPROVEMENTS IN EDUCATION.

" Joseph Lancaster, of the Free School, Borough Road, London, having invented, under the blessing of DIVINE PROVIDENCE, a new and mechanical System of Education, for the use of Schools, feels anxious to disseminate the knowledge of its advantages through the kingdom.

" By this System, paradoxical as it may appear, ABOVE ONE THOUSAND CHILDREN *may be taught and governed by* ONE MASTER ONLY. * * * Any boy, who can read, can teach arithmetic with the certainty of a mathematician, although he knows nothing about it himself.

" It is intended to publish an Abridgment of the System of Education, for the benefit of the poor in Ireland. It will be executed under the inspection of the Author of the original System."—*Star Newspaper*, Feb. 26th, 1807.

On reading this advertisement, the Author instantly wrote to Mr. Whitbread as follows:—

" SIR, *London, 26th February*, 1807.

" In my Newspaper*, the Star, of this date, I have just read, 'Joseph Lancaster, &c., *having invented, under the blessing of Divine Providence, a new and mechanical System of Education, &c.*'

" This advertisement will, I am persuaded, convince you, as fully as it does me, that any personal interview, or conference, on a subject in which the parties differ so widely in point of fact, would only lead to that contradiction, and, perhaps, in the earnestness of disputation, to that altercation, which I am extremely solicitous to avoid, especially with one to whose zeal, industry, perseverance, and matchless address, the mechanical parts of the System, which I have heretofore fondly imagined was my discovery, are under so many obligations, and who, had he stopped here, as once I understood he did, would, as I conceive, have earned universal praise and thanks.

" With great deference I submit to your judgment, whether, not only for the purpose of avoiding altercation, of which I am so solicitous, but also for the sake of that substantial truth, of which I am far more solicitous, any question which you have to put to him, or to me, would not be much more effectually done to your satisfaction in writing?

" It is my anxious wish to give you every information in my power, on a subject on which I have reflected long and much, and studied experimentally; and to do this in the way which, to me, appears least ambiguous and equivocal, and to give every proof of the high consideration with which I have the honour to be, Sir, your obedient Servant, A. BELL."

---

* The Newspaper which the Author took in.

The result of this correspondence was, that Mr. Whitbread, in a subsequent speech, gave a true and correct statement of the facts, which have been related; and on the publication of the substance of his original speech, which was modified accordingly, he subjoined the following note:—

" Dr. Bell, late of the establishment of Fort St. George, in the East Indies . . . . . claims the original invention of the System of Education practised by Mr. Lancaster. So early as the year 1789, he opened a School* at Madras, in which that System was first reduced to practice, with the greatest success, and the most beneficial effects. In the year 1797, he published an *outline*† of his method of instruction, in a small pamphlet, entitled, ' *An Experiment on Education, made at the Male Asylum of Madras.*' That pamphlet has been extended, and very valuable details given to the public, by Dr. Bell, in two subsequent publications, of the years 1805 and 1807. Mr. L.'s Free School, in the Borough, was not opened till the year 1800‡. So that Dr. Bell unquestionably preceded Mr. Lancaster, and to him the world are first indebted for one of the most useful discoveries which has ever been submitted to society."—*Substance of a Speech on the Poor Laws, by S. Whitbread, Esq. M. P.* Feb. 19, 1807. Note, p. 98.

To the same effect was the early criticism of the Edinburgh Review, of October, 1807:—

" We are so far from wishing to undervalue the labours of Dr. Bell, that it gives us great pleasure to express our warmest admiration of what he has done for education. He is unquestionably the *beginner in an art*, which we trust will be carried to a still greater perfection. . . . We hope he will value his deserved reputation above every thing else, and not lose *that originality*, which has brought him into notice."

Such, however, was the effect of a proper name given to the New System, and such the consequence of the Author having all along declined designating it with his own name, and such the support given to this claim, by able and indefatigable advocates and partizans, through diurnal prints, periodical publications, and controversial writings, (in none of which did the Author take

---

* It is usual for certain writers to speak thus of the Asylum at Madras.

† Meaning the Official Report, transmitted to the Court of Directors by the Government of Madras.

‡ It should be 1801, see p. 41, supra.

any share,) that this System has been disseminated
far and wide, under the name of Lancasterian, till, like
America, the error has become so general, that it may
be thought almost too late to correct it. Considering,
however, the peculiar circumstances, and the singular
delusion which has long prevailed, and is still, in a great
degree, prevalent, the Author would be doing injustice
to the work which he has so long and anxiously pro-
secuted, if he did not produce—

CHAP. VIII. *Further Documents corroborative of those
already quoted, and of the Facts which have been stated
relative to the Origin of the Madras System, to its
Character and Results, and to the continuation of its
History to the present time.*

OF the documents, almost innumerable, which may
be adduced to consummate the evidence of this System,
there is room only for brief extracts, from a very few of
such of them as are under the hands of those, whose in-
timate knowledge of the facts they attest, as well as their
impartiality and veracity, do not admit of the slightest
suspicion.

1. An old and valuable friend, who had himself, at
Madras, witnessed the early stages of the New System,
and is still alive, in recommending the establishment of
regimental schools on this system, says:—

" The Male Asylum was, from the time of its institution, till
last year, under the charge of the Rev. Dr. Bell, who declined
receiving either salary or emolument for his trouble. It has
succeeded beyond the most sanguine expectations, and has afforded an opportunity for a learned and ingenious man to
introduce a new mode of teaching and regulation, which he has
lately communicated to the public."—*Plans for the Defence of
Great Britain and Ireland. By Lieutenant Colonel (now General)
Dirom, Deputy-Quarter-Master-General in North Britain. Edinburgh,* 1797.

2. Extract from a New and Appropriate System of
Education, by P. Colquhoun, LL.D. 1806.

" The nation is indebted to the genius, the ability, and per-
severing industry, of the Rev. Dr. Bell, late Superintendent and
Director of the Male Asylum, at Madras, in the East Indies, for
a most enlightened Plan of Education for the poor, which he
some time since disclosed to the public, and for which he deserves
a statue to his memory."

3. Extract of a Letter from Matthew Lewis, Esq., one of the Commissioners of the Royal Military Asylum, at Chelsea.

" Dear Sir, *Devonshire Place, Oct.* 14, 1807.

" Permit me to offer you my cordial thanks for the information and pleasure, which I have derived from the perusal of your Analysis, and for which I hope to have an early opportunity of repeating my acknowledgments to you in person.

" The System of Education, which you have invented, is at once so rational, so simple, and so practicable, that it cannot fail of making its way into general use; and I have infinite gratification in seeing the ROYAL MILITARY ASYLUM, already profiting by your labours, and giving such certain promise of bearing public and powerful evidence of the truth and value of your System.—I am, with real esteem, dear Sir, your faithful humble Servant, M. LEWIS."

" Rev. Dr. Bell.

4. Dr. Barton, Chaplain to the Archbishop of Canterbury, in a sermon preached at Lambeth, for the National School there, says:—" *The* POINT *has been gained, upon which the judicious Instructor may take his stand, and direct the mind in whatever it pleaseth him."*

5. Extract from the Report of the Clergy Orphan School, under the Patronage of Her Majesty. The Right Reverend Lord Bishop of London, President, 1811.

" An important alteration has been made, since the last anniversary Report, in the mode of instruction pursued in the school, by the adoption of the Madras System of Education. This System was invented, as its name imports, in the British East India dominions; and a Report of it, extracted from the Records of the Male Asylum, at Egmore, was, in the year 1796, sent by the Government of Madras, to the Directors of the East India Company, and published *verbatim,* by its Author, on his arrival in Europe, in 1797..... The System was immediately introduced into the parochial school of St. Botolph, Aldgate, by a Trustee of most distinguished and exemplary zeal, for the education of the poor, [D. P. Watts, Esq. of Portland Place;] and about the same time was fully adopted and acted upon at Kendal, by Dr. Briggs, as superintending visitor of the Blue Coat School in that place; and yearly Reports of its complete success were published there, and an account of it appeared in the third volume of the Reports of the Society for bettering the Condition of the Poor..... No plan has yet been proposed, from the general application of which so much and such unmixed good can be expected, as that for which this country, and many other parts of the habitable globe, are indebted to the piety, philanthropy, and unexampled labours, of Dr. Bell."

6. The next extract is from the Barrington School, by Sir Thomas Bernard, Bart. Hatchard, 1812.

" In 1798, the Madras System had, on the suggestion of Mr. D. P. Watts, now of Portland Place, been in some degree adopted in the Charity School of St. Botolph, Aldgate. A few months after, it was established with striking effect, at Kendal, by Dr. Briggs, an eminent physician of that town, since fixed professionally at Liverpool. Reports of the state of this school, induced me to visit it in September, 1800, when I had the pleasure of spending some time with him, and afterwards of giving to the public, in the third volume of our reports [for bettering the condition of the poor, No. 90], a detail of the information I had been able to collect, and the observations which had occurred to me, during three days which I had the pleasure of spending with him, at Kendal. In June, 1801, Mr. Joseph Lancaster opened a large free school in the Borough, in which he adopted a similar mode of tuition.

"I copy the date from Mr. Lancaster's book; but I do not mean to enter into the question, whether Mr. Lancaster borrowed, or did not borrow, from Dr. Bell, the new method of tuition by the pupils themselves; I confine myself to the simple and well-known fact, that the adoption of Dr. Bell's new method, in the Aldgate and Kendal Schools, was prior to the introduction of it into the Borough School."

CHAP. IX.—*Continuation of the Official Documents and Vouchers under the hands of the highest authorities —Recapitulation and Conclusion—Royal Military and Naval Asylums and Schools—the Barrington School —and the National Society.*

§ 1. Army and Navy.

THE complete establishment of the Madras System in the military department, the foundation and endowment of the Barrington School, and the incorporation of the National Society, are circumstances too eventful in the history of the New School, to pass without more particular notice.

Of the first fruits and early promise of the Madras System, on the grandest scale on which it had ever been exhibited, an earnest has been seen, under the hand of one of his Majesty's Commissioners of the Royal Military Asylum, p. 51, supra.

The establishment of REGIMENTAL SCHOOLS on the Madras System stands on supreme authority.

Extract from "*Instructions for establishing and conducting Regimental Schools upon the Rev. Dr. Bell's System, as adopted at the Royal Military Asylum*, Chelsea." Northumberland Court, Strand, London: Printed and Sold BY AUTHORITY, by W. Clowes, November, 1811.

"General Orders.—Horse-Guards, 1st January, 1812.

"With a most earnest desire to give the fullest effect to the benevolent intentions of Government, in favour of the soldiers' children, to which his ROYAL HIGHNESS THE PRINCE REGENT has, in the name and behalf of HIS MAJESTY, given the royal sanction, the COMMANDER-IN-CHIEF calls on all General Officers, Colonels of Regiments, and Commanding Officers of Corps, to take under their special superintendence the Regimental Schools belonging to their respective commands...... With this view, the COMMANDER-IN-CHIEF directs, that the Regimental Schools shall be conducted on military principles; and that, as far as circumstances will permit, their establishment shall be assimilated to that of a regiment, and formed on a System *invented by the Rev. Dr. Bell,* which has been adopted, *with the most complete success, at the* ROYAL MILITARY ASYLUM.

"HIS ROYAL HIGHNESS has directed, that extracts shall be made from " *Dr. Bell's Instructions for conducting a School, through the agency of the Scholars themselves;*" which, having received Dr. Bell's approbation, are subjoined, as the best directions HIS ROYAL HIGHNESS can give for the conduct of the Regimental Schools of the British Army, &c. &c.

"Harry Calvert, Adjutant General."

The introduction of the Madras System into the Navy is recorded by illustrious authorities.

"It has been mentioned, on former occasions, as a subject of high gratification, that this excellent system has, under the illustrious Patronage of His Royal Highness the DUKE OF YORK, been generally introduced into the regiments of the Army. It is now to be stated, as a circumstance no less gratifying, that an opening has been made for its introduction into the Navy, with a fair promise of success."—*Ninth Report of the National Society,* p. 15.

Not long after the adoption of the Madras System into the Military Asylum, it was introduced into the

NAVAL ASYLUM, at Greenwich, where of late it has greatly flourished.

§ 2. *Of the Barrington School.*

The following is a brief record.

" In the year 1801, the Bishop of Durham had appointed Mr. Bernard his Spiritual Chancellor, which occasioned him to make an annual visit to Auckland Castle. During that of 1808, all the arrangements were made for establishing a kind of Collegiate School at Bishop Auckland; not merely for the instruction of young children, but also for preparing the most promising scholars, for the office of schoolmasters, on Dr. Bell's New System of Education. This part of the plan became indispensably necessary, not only for the introduction of the System into the Diocese of Durham, but also its extension into every other, as the Central School in the metropolis was not at that time established. Applications were therefore made at the Barrington School, and complied with, for supplying the Dioceses of Carlisle, Exeter, York, and Winchester, with instructors, which could not then be obtained elsewhere. For the perpetual support of this noble establishment, the Bishop of Durham settled, by deed, upon four trustees, a sum of money in the funds, producing four hundred and thirty-six pounds a year. He also erected, at his own expense, a spacious and elegant stone building, on a plan by Mr. Bernard, which was opened for the school, 26th of May, 1810, being his Lordship's birth-day."—*Extract from the Life of Sir Thomas Bernard, by the Rev. James Baker, his nephew and executor, pp.* 89, 90.

It is with extreme regret that the Author is under the indispensable necessity (for reasons already assigned), to suppress numerous official reports of the earliest, as well as latest, exhibitions of the Madras System, in public and private institutions, hospitals, parochial, endowed, and free-schools, in England and Wales, which he has recorded in Elements of Tuition, Parts 1, 2, and 3. And in the former edition of Instructions, &c.: to the Founders, Patrons, and Visitors of which he can never too often repeat his estimation and obligation.

§ 3. *National Society.*

Let the National Society speak the rest. That the system of education which, in the beginning, went forth under the signature and recommendation of the highest authorities abroad, may, in the conclusion, rest on the experience and sanction of the highest authorities at home.

The following are extracts from the first Annual Report, 1812, of the General Committee.

P. 25. " The Committee beg leave previously to observe, that the adoption of the Madras System by the Society, has proceeded from the experience, not only of the facility by which this system. communicates instruction, but of the influence which hitherto it is found to have on the morals of the children."

P. 18. " The. facility of communicating instruction by the System now intended to be brought into general use; its efficiency in fixing the attention, and in inculcating the things taught; the eagerness, and even delight, with which the children embrace it; the entire possession which it takes of their minds, so as to render them pliant and obedient to discipline, (all of which is visible to any one who visits the schools lately instituted on this plan;) and the anxiety which their parents shew to have them instructed, are powerful instruments both for infusing into their minds good knowledge, and forming them to good habits. The economy with which, after the first formation of proper schools, it may be conducted, is also such as to give us reason to hope, that the very lowest classes of society may receive the benefit of it, and that it may become universal."

P. 56. " In all the Reports of the schools established through the assistance of the Society, the Committee have the pleasure of observing, that the happiness of the children, under this plan of education, forms a prominent subject of remark.

" To those who have observed the interest which is created where the spirit of emulation is constantly in action, and who know the result of the full employment of the mind, this can occasion no surprise. It is, in truth, the natural consequence of the new system: but the Committee would be inexcusable, if they did not bring forward this subject to the notice of the public; because they are persuaded, that it must be most gratifying to all the supporters of the Institution, to learn, that, in this method of instruction, *pleasure and improvement* accompany each other, and that by the same act of benevolence, they are forming the minds, and promoting the cheerfulness of the children under their protection."

The Seventh Annual Report of the National Society, 1819, *closes with these words:*

" Being fully sensible that the more they can plant this admirable system with deep and strong roots in every part of the kingdom, the more they will advance the cause of true religion, and promote the solid welfare of the state; together with the happiness, present and eternal, of those individuals, to whom its blessings are extended."

*The Conclusion of the Third Report of the General
Committee of the National Society,* dated 1814, will not
be considered as an unsuitable conclusion to these notes,
proofs, and illustrations.

P. 29. " Of the debt of gratitude due to Dr. Bell, for devising,
and bringing to maturity, a method of general education, which
has enabled the Governors of the Church to execute what our
Reformers projected—the giving to the whole population of the
realm, a competent measure of useful learning, seasoned with
religious instruction, in the principles of our national faith—the
Committee feel that it is quite out of date for them to offer any
computation. The system itself, now extended into almost every
part of the empire, has carried with it the only adequate exempli-.
fication of the pretensions of its inventor. But it would be a
failure of duty in the General Committee, not to advert to the new
and increasing obligations which he is conferring, not merely on
the Society, but on the nation at large. Possessing an honourable
retirement, he might deem himself exonerated, by his past services, from farther exertion; but, with unabated zeal, and at his
own charges, he continues to dedicate his whole time, and all the
energies of his mind, to the great work which he has begun;
dividing the year between his attendance at the Central School,
and the visitation of its numerous country connexions, and
apparently setting no other value upon his life, than as he can
render it instrumental to the universal adoption of the Madras
System. These are deservings, which the General Committee
deem it incumbent on them to record, but do not pretend to
estimate.

" Here they would close their Report, if they did not deem it
of importance to let it be known to the public, that the conduct
and management of the Institution, has never ceased to engage
the consideration of many of the first characters, both of Church
and State, who have been selected for that purpose by the
Society at large. It would be superfluous to enumerate, individually, all those whose exertions have been eminently serviceable;
but it must be satisfactory to the public to learn, and therefore it is their duty not to withhold the fact, that, notwithstanding
the numerous and various demands on the time of THEIR MOST
REVEREND PRESIDENT, the ARCHBISHOP OF CANTERBURY, the
Society has never failed to receive the countenance of his high
authority, as well by his constantly presiding at all their deliber-
ations, as by his presence at the public examinations of the
children at the Central School. It is thus that life and energy
have been diffused through all parts of the Institution; and that
within two years from its establishment, it has risen from

inconsiderable beginning to that high consideration, in which the General Committee have the satisfaction to know that it is now universally held by the benevolent and discerning inhabitants of this enlightened empire."

Finally, to sum up the whole—

" It is not matter of doubtful speculation; it is proved and confirmed, by the growing experience of every day, that, of all the means which can be adopted for the counteraction of baneful principles, and for the dissemination of good, the education of the rising generation, according to the National System, is the most effectual; that, by following this plan, we build up the surest and most impregnable barrier against the designs of the infidel and the disaffected; lay the firm ground-work of public and private happiness, and combine the purpose of true benevolence with that of an enlightened and liberal policy."—*Ninth Report of the National Society*, 1820.

PART II.
On the Madras System of Education.

" As emulation is especially serviceable in fostering the studies of those who have made some proficiency in learning; so beginners and novices find greater benefit, as well as satisfaction, from imitating their school-fellows than their master, because the one is far easier than the other."—QUIN.

CHAP. I.—*Object of elementary Education.*

To render simple, easy, pleasant, expeditious, and economical the acquisition of the rudiments of letters, morality, and religion, are the leading objects of elementary education. It has accordingly been the study of the Author of this Essay, through the instrumentality of a new *Organ*, to combine, in harmonious union, the progress and amusement of the scholar, the ease and satisfaction of the master, and the interest and gratification of the parent. In a word, to render a school in reality a " *ludus literarius*"—*a game of letters*—in which the profit and amusement of its pupils go hand in hand.

Such is the immediate, or proximate object, of the New System. Its ultimate object, the ultimate object and end of all education, is to make GOOD SUBJECTS, GOOD MEN, GOOD CHRISTIANS * :" in other words, to promote the temporal and spiritual welfare of its pupils—

* Page 50.
E

objects, which, in my mind, do not admit of being separated.*

To attain these ends,—to attain any good end in education, the grand desideratum is, *to fix attention, to call forth exertion, to prevent the waste of time in school.*

Referring to the Report of the Military Asylum at Madras, in which, as has been seen, the New System of Education originated, for the complete success of the first experiment (of which a specimen has been given above), and which has not, perhaps, in respect of the entire result, been since surpassed, it is here proposed to expound the general laws, and detail the arrangements, by which this *universal and immutable System of Mutual Instruction and Moral Discipline* is carried into effect, in the Central, and other well-conducted schools of the National Society.

CHAP. II. — *Scheme of a School on the Madras, or National System.*

1. The entire *Economy†* of a Madras School is conducted by a single master, or superintendent, *through the agency of the scholars themselves.* For this purpose,

2. The school is arranged into forms, or classes, each composed of members, who have made a similar proficiency; and are occasionally paired off into tutors and pupils, the superior being tutors to the inferior boys.

3. The scholar ever finds his level, by a constant competition with his fellows, and rises and falls in his place in the class, and in the forms of the school, according to his relative proficiency.

4. To each class are attached a teacher, and, if numerous, an assistant teacher; who are perpetually present

---

* "It was my chief object, in raising my young teachers, to carry into effect the intentions of the honourable Court of Directors (when they ordered this establishment to be formed), in such a manner as might be most *conducive to their views, to the interests of this government, to the benefit of society, and to the good of the pupils committed to my charge; all of which objects have been, and are so blended together in my mind, that I cannot separate them even in imagination.*" p. 49.

† By *economy*, when printed in italics, I denote economy, not only in its common acceptation of frugality of expense, but also in its classical and proper sense, as comprehending the entire internal regulation, arrangement, order, and government of the *household;*—the entire instruction and discipline of the school, in all its departments.

with their class, and are responsible for its order, behaviour, diligence, and improvement. In large schools, an usher or superior teacher is set over every three or four classes, and a head usher over the whole.

5. Monitors are appointed to the charge of the books, slates, pencils, paper, pens, ink, and of the various departments and offices of the school-room.

6. In charity, free, or other schools, supported by endowment, or voluntary contribution, there often presides over all, as in old times, a superintendent, or chaplain, or one of the trustees, directors, or visitors, whose province is to inspect, regulate, and control the scholastic machine in all its departments.

What goes before properly constitutes the Madras System of Education, or the machinery of the new School—as founded on *Self-Tuition*, or *Mutual Instruction*. What follows is for the purpose of ensuring accuracy and precision, and for checks and instruments of Discipline.

7. The daily lessons are marked in the teacher's books: and Registers are kept of admission; and of the progress of each class, and of the relative and individual proficiency of each scholar.

8. If any gross misdemeanour should occur, the accused is tried by a jury of his peers, and the sentence is inflicted, mitigated, or remitted, at the discretion of the superintendent, visitor, or master. But, when the laws of the school are duly administered, there will hardly ever be occasion for this instrument of discipline.

Such, in brief, is the scheme of a Madras School, wherein the *System hinges entirely on the tuition by the scholars themselves.*

CHAP III.—*On the Classification of a School.*

" With what joy are boys elated when they come off victors? With what shame are they covered when vanquished? With what solicitude do they exert themselves, not to incur blame? With what eagerness do they seek to earn praise? What toils do they not undergo, that they may be chief among their fellows?"—CICERO.

In order to carry into effect the System of Education, the scheme of which has been exhibited in the foregoing

Chapter, the *first and grand law*, as has been stated, is, that *every scholar finds for himself his level, and unceasingly rises and falls in his place in the form, and in the ranks of the school, according to his relative performance.*

For this, as well as other important purposes, it is requisite to arrange the school into classes. The arrangement is made according to the proficiency of the scholars, from the first or highest, to the last or lowest, form.

The classes may, on an average, consist of about thirty-six scholars, if so many are on a footing of equality. The higher classes are often more, and the lower less, numerous. The fewer the classes, and the greater the number of members in each, the better; for, in the same ratio, are the facility of instruction, inspection, and superintendence, the scope of imitation and emulation, and the option of able and expert teachers.*

The form of the class is sometimes circular, or rectangular, but oftener square, three sides of which are occupied, each by one third of the number of scholars, who are arranged at equal distances from one another, and the fourth by the master, teacher, or visitor. But, whatever be the form, it is generally called the circle on the floor.

For the equalization of the classes, in point of proficiency, the scholar, who has held a high place in his class for some time, is promoted to the class above, and is placed at the bottom; but if, on trial, he proves unequal to his new class-fellows, he must revert to his former class; and the boy who fails, for some time, after due warning and trial, in saying his daily lessons, is degraded to the class below, and is placed at the head; but if he proves superior to his new associates, he then resumes his former class, on a new trial.

The best method, however, of maintaining *equalized*†

* When, as often occurs, instead of thirty-six, the classes are formed of six scholars each, six able teachers are wanted instead of one; the task of superintendence and inspection on the part of the masters and visitors, and the risque of neglect in this necessary office, is multiplied sixfold; and the advantages of imitation and emulation are diminished almost in the same proportion.

† Classes composed of scholars who have made equal progress.

classes, is by continually feeding the higher from the lower, whereby the unpleasant necessity of degrading the scholars inferior in genius or progress, may, in a great measure, if not entirely, be dispensed with.

When, in learning, or saying, or rehearsing, a lesson on the floor, a boy fails or errs, the next below, or, after a few seconds, any other in succession who prompts him, takes, of his own accord, the place above him, and all between; and if he do not then repeat what has been told, he is, in like manner, again corrected. If all below fail, the head boy is referred to; but if he also fail, any one who now prompts, takes the head of the class. The next to the defaulter, and one only, in his turn, must speak at a time. The scholar who prompts before his turn, or, if above the reader, till the head boy has been appealed to, forfeits a place.*

These simple laws keep every one on the alert, as well above as below the speaker, all being liable, on every mistake, to lose a place.

In writing and cyphering, &c., whether at the desk, or on the floor, let each scholar be invariably arranged according to his daily performance.

A class, which is not perfectly master of the book they have gone through, by being joined to an inferior class, and revising it with them, will bring them forward at the same time that they still more improve themselves; and the whole, or a great proportion of the members of an inferior class, deservedly promoted to a superior, will soon rise to the level of their new associates, from imitation, emulation, and excited diligence; and boys of superior parts, will generally attain a high station in their new class.

In all cases, the scholars promoted are required (on the penalty of forfeiting their preferment) to overtake, by private, as well as public study, in those branches in which they are inferior, their new class-fellows.

Every new scholar, whatever his former progress may have been, is placed at the bottom of the school, and

* In going to a higher place in the class the scholar walks before, and to a lower, behind his fellows.

works his way up through the classes, learning the practices and rules of the school as he goes along, till he finds his appropriate station. It is thus that the dunces, as they are called, from other schools, are no longer dunces when they enter a Madras School.

By these means, no class is ever retarded by idle or dull boys, and every boy, in every class, is fully and profitably employed; and by thus finding his own level, his improvement is most effectually promoted, and rendered a *maximum.* Conscious that his lot depends upon his own exertion, and his relative attainments; and that, whether he rises or falls in the ranks of the school, he is in his proper place; he recognises the justice, perceives the fitness, and feels the utility, of rules so happily conducive to the general weal.

In a word: By this classification—which, though not entirely new, nor peculiar to the Madras School, is yet carried to an extent there, which renders it, in a great degree, new—a teacher has no more trouble, nay, has less trouble, in the tuition of a whole class, than of a single scholar; and that emulation, or desire of excellence, which the Creator has implanted in the infant breast, for the wisest and noblest purposes, is thus called forth, and proves a perpetual source of amusement, and an unceasing incentive to laudable exertion.

Further fruits of this classification, will be seen in the next Chapter.

CHAP. IV.— *On the Discipline of the School,— its Rewards, and Punishments.*

" The whipping of boys I cannot endure, though the practice is common, and is not disapproved of by Chrysippus. * * * Lastly, if AN ASSIDUOUS EXACTOR OF STUDIES watch over the scholar, there will be no need of this CASTIGATION (chastisement.) But as matters now stand, through the negligence of the pedagogue (tutor), boys seem to be so corrected, that they are not constrained to do their duty, but punished for not doing it*."—QUIN.

§ 1. *On the appropriate Rewards and Punishments of the Madras School.*

It is gratifying to observe, that the great master of antiquity was aware of the efficacy of one of the instruments of discipline and learning employed in a Madras

* See *Ludus Literarius,* p. 170.

School; and, while the Author anticipates the opinions, the sentiments, and the actual practice of future ages, with unshaken and growing conviction, from the earnest he has already had in the issue of his former anticipations, he frequently indulges in the pleasing reflection, how the ablest and most practical writer, on the subject of education, would have been delighted, if he had seen the day, when a simple discovery, of which he seems to have had a glimpse, has furnished, to an extent far beyond what he had contemplated, *assiduous exactors of studies*, for the double purpose of instruction and discipline.

The entire machinery of the New School, is fitted to prevent idleness and offences, to call forth diligence and exertion, and thereby to supersede the flagellation, which he so justly reprobated.

Simultaneously, and by the same means that it conducts the instruction, it conducts also the moral, religious, and intellectual discipline of its pupils.

Corporeal punishment has no tendency, of itself, to sharpen the wit, improve the memory, or advance the knowledge of the patient. On the other hand, it frequently serves only to harden the offender, disgust his school-fellows, beget a hatred of the school, the book, and the master, and thereby defeat its own end. The discipline, which depends on bodily fear, fails, whenever there is the hope of escaping detection; and, at best, has seldom more than a temporary effect, which often ceases with the pain it inflicts. Under its dominion, the scholar aims only at impunity, and not at improvement or reformation.

Instead, therefore, of arbitrary and occasional inflictions, the Madras System has substituted a code of laws, unceasing in operation, founded on the constitution of man, adapted to the genius of children, and left to the administration of its subjects; or, as might almost be said, to execute themselves.

1. In the first place, the continual presence and vigilance of the teachers, with their respective classes, serve, in an obvious and eminent manner, to prevent offences and disorder, idleness and inattention, and to secure the incessant occupation of the scholars.

.2. In the next place, the motives and inducements, which the Madras System comprehends within itself, take a strong hold on the infant mind, and have a powerful operation in producing diligence and exertion, which are never suffered to flag.

3. The portions of honour and shame, which of itself it continually distributes, with an impartial and unerring hand, form the most appropriate and efficient rewards of the meritorious, and, at the same time, the most rational and powerful correctives of the undeserving. The promotion of the one, and the degradation of the other, immediately consequent upon, and in just proportion to, their deserts, are the simple and powerful stimulants, most efficacious in the government, as well as the instruction of a school.

In short, the law of *equalized* classification, renders a school an *arena*, in which rewards and punishments are every moment assigned to the scholastic combatants, according to their good or ill success.

" To be *dux* of a class, is a prize of no small value." How much more is the laudable ambition of youth, fired by the desire of rising to a higher class; and his exertion stimulated, by the apprehension of being degraded to a lower class.

Again: besides these immediate fruits of the new classification, it furnishes the teacher with a ready instrument for correcting various errors, and reforming defaulters. In every case of failure, irregularity, or aggression, such as low utterance, reading fast, or in a drawling or singing tone, indistinct articulation, being unsteady, inattentive, holding down the head, not standing upright, or in the proper place, the teacher has only to point to, or name, the culprit, and he goes down a place, and then, if need be, another, &c.; but if he fail grossly, or wittingly misbehaves, he is turned down, according to the nature of his offence, two or more places, or even to the bottom of the class: when unruly or disobedient, he is detained there for some time. If still refractory, he is degraded to a lower class; so also with late boys, truants, and other defaulters. The loss of more than one place, being attached to any offence, will, in a well regulated school, be sensibly felt by the tender mind; and the forfeiture of a class, makes a deep impression, and calls forth the utmost efforts to wipe out the disgrace, and regain the lost honours.

In brief, it is a maxim of the New School, fully ascertained by experience, that a *maximum* of improvement cannot be obtained, without a *minimum** of punishment. The nice sensibility and delicacy of feeling which is produced by mild and gentle treatment, have no small influence on the character and conduct of the pupils.

§ 2. *On the extra Rewards and Punishments of the New School.*

Besides these intrinsic and appropriate stimulants of improved classification, which have been just described, and which will, in almost every case, be found sufficient, if duly administered, the New School has, on extraordinary occasions, which do not fall under the law of promotion and degradation, recourse to expedients of a different description, as in common use.

In regard to punishments, such are confinement under monitors at extra hours, to recover, by diligence, what has been lost by absence, &c., and, " horresco referens," solitary confinement; and, in extreme cases, if such, after all, should occur, expulsion—a fatal and deplorable issue, which every possible means should be employed to obviate.

Indeed, the spirit of the whole school, when duly directed, renders such cases of so rare occurrence, as scarcely to require a separate provision.

In short, scarcely can an offence be committed; for the teacher or monitor is always at hand to prevent it, or, if committed, escape instant detection, and immediate correction. For any transgression, which may require solemn animadversion, the teacher reports the culprit to the master. If the teacher neglect this duty, he is himself amenable for the penalty, which his pupil had incurred; and, on any flagrant neglect or misrule, the teacher forfeits his station or post.†

* A master being asked, by what means a young child, in his school, had made so extraordinary a progress, answered, " I am always cheerful with him."

† In such cases resort was wont to be had to a jury of good boys;

When tickets are given for Rewards, the forfeiture of those which the boys have obtained, or the withholding of them for a time from those who are in the habit of earning them, is a common punishment for any venial neglect or trespass.

There remains only the pleasing task of recording the extra Rewards or premiums in common use.

Some of these are tickets of merit for regular attendance, and good behaviour, at Church, and at School, which have a double effect. The scholars, who on the day of reckoning cannot produce the due number of tickets, while they lose the reward, feel ashamed and disgraced. On the contrary, they who bring them, while they receive the allotted reward, have a consciousness of desert in their earnings, which is truly gratifying, and all are stimulated to regularity, and good conduct, in future. These Tickets are sometimes exchanged for others of greater value, which last are set at $\frac{1}{2}d.$ or $1d.$ the half-dozen.

Teachers are rewarded, not by a fixed stipend, which is liable to fail of its object, but according to their deserts, their own good conduct, and the attendance, behaviour and improvement of their respective classes.

These Rewards are either honorary or pecuniary. In some schools, medals, books, clothes, &c. are given at the (quarterly, or half-yearly, or) annual examination, to the teachers, and sometimes to the scholars, who are eminently distinguished by their proficiency, and meritorious conduct. It is expedient that the pecuniary rewards to teachers be distributed once a week after the examination. A small portion is given in hand, and the greater part is put into a fund book, to accumulate for them, till, at a proper age and attainments, they quit school with leave, and without having forfeited these rewards by misbehaviour, or misconduct. At some schools, fund books are converted into saving banks, and, at others, saving banks are established.

It is only justice to children to say, that they are not so much alive to any reward, as to the advantages they enjoy in the speedy and perfect instruction, under the mild, but inflexible, laws of the New School: and that

but in the course of experience, in well-regulated schools, this has been so seldom necessary, as to become almost, if not altogether, a dead letter.

no rewards are so acceptable to good teachers, or more appropriate, than aiding and assisting them in carrying on their own studies, at extra hours, and at home.

CHAP. V.—*On perfect Instruction and Order.*

The second main law of a Madras School is, that its instruction be conducted in a gradually progressive course of study, by short, easy, adapted, and perfect lessons, " a notioribus ad minus nota."

The law of Classification, treated of in a former Chapter, goes a great way, when duly executed, to the accomplishment of this important object.

In some schools, one or more boys may be masters of the lesson, others partially acquainted with it, and others totally ignorant of it. Nay, a majority of the scholars may pass through the forms of the school, and yet acquire little or nothing of what is there taught. This is the case when the lessons prescribed are beyond their reach, and they are unable to overtake their daily tasks; or when they have the option to prefer idleness or play, and the risk of being flogged, to the exercise of mind and the acquisition of letters.

Such cannot happen in a Madras School, where the scholar ranks not according to his seniority or standing, but to his proficiency, and actual attainments; and where no lesson is assigned beyond his abilities, or passed over without being learnt.

One of the maxims of the Madras Asylum was, in the language there spoken, that " a boy cannot do any thing right the first time; but that he must learn, when he sets about it, by means of *his teacher,* so as to be able to do it himself ever after*." In other words, the rule is, that each successive lesson, and practice, be made at once familiar to the scholars, before another is taken in hand; and that, in every act and every movement, whether in walking in and out of school, taking places at the writing desk, or in classes on the floor, the utmost order, regularity, and good conduct be observed.

In particular, let attention be paid to the initiatory lessons, the neglect of which not only prevents the

* Page 42.

scholar from acquiring for years, what may be learned in
months, but, by the habits it begets, opposes no small
obstacle to his future studies.

In the beginning, therefore, never prescribe a lesson,
or task, which the scholar can require more than ten
minutes, or a quarter of an hour, to learn.   Never omit
marking the book the moment the lesson is given out;
nor quit a letter, a word, a line, or a verse, or a sentence,
or a paragraph, or a section, or a chapter, or a book, or a
task of any kind, till the learner is acquainted with it.

In the daily repetition by heart, let every scholar be
taught to rehearse prayers, graces, catechism, &c., in the
style and tone of a good reader, which all will soon be
able to do, while the organs are pliant, by imitation, as
they unceasingly repeat them with their instructors and
fellows; and if the same rule be observed, in regard to
the first paragraph and section, in beginning to read, a
better manner may be acquired in a few lessons, than is
often attained while at school, under a vitious or faulty
tone.

Let the master himself, then, watch over the uniform
execution of these directions; not satisfying himself by
telling the teacher to do so and so, but by doing it, in
the first instance, with and for him, and shewing him
how to do it, and seeing it done.

The advantage of perfect instruction will be understood,
by remarking how much of the difficulty of learning to
read is gradually done away, by removing every obstacle
on its first occurrence; of which, specimens may be seen
in the stops and points, which occur in every sentence,
and in those words of most frequent use, of which it is
said three or four score, counted every time they occur,
amount to one half the number of words in any book.
The same observation applies to the construction and
analysis of sentences, owing to the similarity among them.
One lesson perfectly learned, the next is in part known,
and a habit of attention and accuracy, which is of no
small importance, is acquired.

As in many schools there is much waste of time, occasioned by passing slightly over what is most important,
and unknown; so is there in others, by repeating and

dwelling on what is less material, and already well known. The true art of tuition consists in tasking the abilities of the scholars sufficiently to maintain a perpetual interest, and call forth a moderate exercise of the faculties of the mind, which is no less grateful than the moderate stretch of the muscles of the body; and by not imposing on them burdens beyond what they are readily able to bear: Perfect instruction, in a progressive course of study, by the love of knowledge natural to man, and of novelty (the great parent of pleasure, especially to children,) renders a school a perpetual source of enjoyment to the infant mind. This not only renders study pleasurable at the time, but also no less so on reflection, by the pleasurable emotions with which it is associated.

As, on the one hand, the scholar has a pleasure in doing what he can perfectly perform, and perfectly understand, so, on the other hand, every task is irksome to him, which is above his comprehension, or in which he is not duly instructed.

In short, when the law of perfect instruction, and perfect order is duly executed, there is only one thing to be learned at a time, and all is ease, despatch, and pleasure. When neglected, in the first instance, which is the fatal error in many schools, a complication of difficulties and bad habits is formed, which it is extremely toilsome to unravel. All that has been imperfectly learned or done, must be unlearned and undone, and a commencement made anew, on a correct and regular method. The accumulation of ill habits and ill practices can only be diminished one by one, and one by one right habits and right practices substituted in their stead. These scholastic knots cannot be cut; they must be untied. In teaching and implanting habits *ab initio*, there is no difficulty. The difficulty lies in unlearning and in undoing bad habits, which indulged become a second nature.

It would be wrong to conclude this Chapter, without warning preceptors of a rock, on which they are liable to split. It is not unusual for masters, after having exhibited, in every department of their school, no bad specimen of the Madras System of Education, when they

F

observe, that visitors are in general satisfied with the
inspection or examination of the upper forms, to content
themselves also, with the exhibition of the higher classes,
(who can, and for the most part do, carry on their own
tuition,) to the neglect of the lower classes, where the
task of teaching is less pleasant, and requires their
minute inspection and superintendence. Hence the
teachers of the lower classes become dissatisfied and
supine, and fall off, in proportion to the inattention which
they experience. Their classes, in rising to the superior
forms, prove greatly inferior to their predecessors in
habits and attainments; and the whole school undergoes
a revolution, and forfeits its character, and, in no small
degree, its usefulness.

Seeing, then, that what constitutes the main difference
between one school and another, is perfect and imperfect
instruction, I cannot forbear repeating here, once more,
an observation, which it is my most anxious wish, as it
has always been my most earnest endeavour, to inculcate.
Let no master, as he values the satisfaction and approbation of the visitors and directors of his school, the
profit and delight of his pupils, the gratification of their
parents and friends, and the good opinion of the public,
and his own ease and comfort, think he has done his
duty, while there is a single child in his school, who is
not a good scholar, who is not perfectly instructed in
every lesson, as he goes along. But let it also be
remembered, that the scholar's time must not be idly
spent in repeating again and again, what is already
familiar to him, except as far as may be requisite to
prevent its being forgotten.

Chap. VI.—*On the Master and Teachers.*

§ 1. *On the functions of the Master.*

In the Report of the Madras Asylum, it is said of the
superintendent (or master), that " His scrutinizing eye
must pervade the whole system,—his active mind must
give it energy,—and his unbiassed judgment, and equal
justice, must maintain the general order and harmony."
p. 42.

The same remark applies to the visitors, whom it
behoves to be conversant, as well with the practice, as

with the theory, of the New School, in order to enable them to perform their office with effect, to instruct, assist, and support the master, in the due exercise of those functions, which, when there is no superintendent or visitor, he has alone to perform.

In speaking of individual scholars, who happen to fall under his (the master's) particular cognizance, it is said, " He is to encourage the diffident, the timid, and the backward,—to check and repress the forward and presumptuous,—to rouse and animate the indolent and phlegmatic,—and to bestow just and ample commendation upon the diligent, attentive, and orderly, however dull their capacity, or slow their progress. In short, he is to deal out praise and dispraise, encouragement and warning, according to the temper, disposition, and genius of the scholar."

Happily, however, the performance of these functions is not left to such individual acts as are liable to error, or to be neglected. Much more certain a provision is made for their due execution. The fact is, that the general laws of the New School are, by their immediate operation and influence, sufficient of themselves, for the accomplishment of the objects, which have been mentioned.

It is, therefore, the master's unceasing duty, to direct, guide, and control the uniform and impartial execution of these laws, in all the departments of the school, so as to render them effectual to the purposes for which they are framed. These are to maintain quiet and order—to give full scope to the love of imitation, and spirit of emulation, so as to promote diligence and delight—advance the general progress—imbue the infant mind with the first principles of morality and religion—and implant, in the tender heart, habits of method, order, and piety.

For this purpose, he must never fail to inspect, examine, and assist in instructing the classes, one by one, and occupy himself wherever there is most occasion for his services, and where they will best tell. He should ever and anon, with his watch in his hand, attend the teacher of each class when the lesson is given out, learned, and said, and, according to the ability of the scholars, apportion its length. He must not expect that his school will ever rise to eminence, or long continue in that state, unless he himself ascertains how much each class can advance in a given time, and exact the performance accordingly.

Such are the means by which the master will fully acquit himself of the important duties committed to him—advance the welfare of the rising generation—of the society to which they belong—and, as far as depends on him, of their common country.

§ 2. *On the Master's selection and management of the Teachers, and on their functions.*

" As the judge of the people is himself, so are his officers; and what manner of man the ruler of the city is, such are all they that dwell therein." Ecclus. x. 2.

" The great advantage of the system is, that you have *a teacher and an assistant for every class.*" p. 41.

In the former section it has been said, that it is the indispensable duty of the master to ascertain that every lesson is adapted and apportioned to the capacity of every scholar, and is perfectly learned and understood. The new power, which the system of Mutual Tuition puts into his hands, furnishes him with ample leisure and means for the performance of this important duty. When not actually present himself, he is virtually so, by his faithful ministers, with every child, every moment of time. The teachers and assistants, to whom, under his vigilant superintendence, the charge of each class is committed, are responsible to him for its instruction and discipline, and for the happiness, progress, orderly behaviour, and good conduct of their pupils. It is with them, through them, and by them, including the general assistance of his usher, or ushers, who act immediately under him, that he has to conduct all the operations of the school; and his agents will ever be such as he makes them—good, bad, or indifferent. As he forms them, so will they form their classes. The maxim of the Madras School is, " *Whatever the master is, such are his scholars; and that there can be but one dunce and one fault in a school.*"

It is, then, of the utmost importance to select, for his ushers, teachers, and monitors, the most intelligent, able, and active scholars, whom he can command and rely upon, for the faithful and zealous performance of the trust committed to them. The selection is easily made in a school, where talent is sure to shew itself in characters, that he who runs can read. If, in the beginning, the master be not acquainted with the dispositions and abilities of his pupils, the option may be confided to the elective voice of the superior classes, or head boys, who are always well acquainted with the qualifications of their school-fellows. The master's next duty is, to direct, guide, and assist his teachers in the instruction and discipline of their respective classes, himself, in the first instance, if necessary, performing their offices *seriatim* for and with them, and thereby qualifying them to take the charge upon themselves.

The youthful teachers, when judiciously selected, well instructed, and duly superintended, will perform their functions with greater zeal, energy, and perseverance, than adult ushers, or even than the master himself. They do not tire (for which we have the authority of Quintilian, as well as daily experience) like men, in continually doing the same thing. They are exalted by that office, which the adult usher feels as a degradation. They can be displaced, and others substituted in their stead, as often as there is occasion. They are tractable, and, in the hands of a master who is acquainted with the disposition and genius of children, and knows how to treat them, or, which is the same thing, will literally conform to the laws prescribed to him, they place their happiness in doing for him whatever he listeth; sensible that whatever, in the just administration of the rules of the school, he commands, will most effectually contribute to their own welfare and improvement, as well as to that of their pupils. In such hands, not only do none of those vices, which speculative writers and talkers are wont to ascribe to the principles of the Madras School, ever shew themselves; but, on the other hand, the opposite virtues are eminently conspicuous. The common concern, which all the members of the school feel in its general *economy,* naturally leads them to take a reciprocal interest in one another; and they do take that interest accordingly.

After all, however, it is absolutely requisite that the master exert his utmost vigilance and discretion, in overlooking all his ushers and teachers, and in preventing, or in stopping, on its first occurrence, the smallest irregularity, or deviation from rule. At no time must he relax his exertions in superintending his ministers, supporting their authority, stimulating their endeavours, and advancing the growing progress of their classes. If he fail, in the first instance, from incompetency, indolence, want of zeal, or any other cause, duly to qualify his ministers, and to put their respective classes in order for and by them, his school will never flourish; or if, after having qualified them, and brought his school into a respectable state, he become remiss, which frequently happens, in watching over, regulating, and controlling every operation, it is certain that there will be a proportionate falling* off in the order, improvement, happiness, and good conduct of his scholars. On the other hand, he will see the manifestation and reward of his faithful and diligent services, in the number, attendance, and progress of his scholars.

While the teacher is occupied with the instruction of the class, it is more especially the business of the assistant teacher to attend to the general order, to keep the boys steady in their classes, standing upright, at equal distances from one another, holding up, and intent on, their books, or slates, and repeating, and also, in the lower classes, pointing at whatever is said or read, by themselves or their class-fellows. The same attention must be paid to their sitting and behaviour at their desks, or on the benches.

---

* This position is confirmed by the experience of nearly thirty years. When at the Madras Asylum, it was officially reported to me, " that the boys were all of them so familiar with, and so instructed in, the system, and felt it so well calculated *to promote their welfare, to advance their learning, and to preclude punishment*, that they did not require looking after, as they of themselves habitually performed their daily tasks." My remark at the time was, " But this must be received with a grain of allowance, as I have ever observed that the *smallest inattention to the preservation of any part of the system, occasions a proportionate falling off*." p. 32.

: The teachers should be retained in their station as long as they perform their task with ability and success, and is consistent with the general good, and no longer. Objects of honourable emulation should be held up to them. They should be fully impressed with the natural and necessary advantages of their station. *That the teacher profits far more by teaching than the scholar does by learning,* is a received maxim of great antiquity, which all experience confirms — " Docemur docendo." — " He, who teaches, learns." Roger Ascham, the able preceptor of Queen Elizabeth, was wont to say that " a boy learned more from giving a lecture to another in *Cordery,* than by receiving one himself in *Homer.*". The words of Lilye, to this effect, ought to be engraven on the walls of every school :—

> " Qui docet indoctos, licet indoctissimus esset,
> Ipse brevi reliquis doctior esse queat."

Indeed, in most schools, even not on the Madras System, the scholars are, perhaps, more improved by what they teach themselves, or learn from one another, than from the lectures of the master. How much more so, then, in a Madras school, where teachers are unceasingly employed in the instruction of their fellows; and where they themselves say every lesson, and perform every task, with their class, and are thus improved by their own practice, as well as by the act of teaching, while the scholars are furnished with a model for imitation, of which the tender mind is ever apt to avail itself. Add to this, that it is felt and acknowledged, that the act of teaching serves, in an eminent degree, as an apprenticeship to qualify for active employment, for business, and affairs.

Besides, it is an easy matter for the master to give books and tasks to his teachers, who are advanced considerably beyond the class of which they have charge, to enable them to carry on their own studies at home, and at leisure hours, without interfering with the discharge of their daily offices in school.

An able master finds no difficulty in selecting and retaining teachers. An incompetent master may be known by his failure in this respect: the master who performs

his duty faithfully, gains the hearts of his scholars, and
can direct their energies as he sees fit.   From his pupils
his influence extends to their parents, who are completely
won by their being made sensible of the happiness and
improvement of their children.   The careless and unequal
master has no weight, either with his pupils, or their
parents, who are alike aware of his insufficiency, or mis-
government.   He is sure to betray himself by his constant
complaining of the badness of his teachers, and of his
scholars, and of the troublesomeness of their parents:
and cannot be made sensible that the fault lies solely
with himself, and that, were his school in able hands, the
reverse of all this would be the case: and that the children, who were pointed out as the most refractory and
troublesome, will often, under better management, become the most orderly and exemplary. This is no ideal
case, but matter of fact, which has been often brought to
the test.

In some schools, a double, or even treble, set of teachers are employed, which is thought to excite diligence
and emulation, and furnishes them with more time for
carrying on their own studies.   In other schools, the
candidate for preferment is appointed to teach a junior
class, and his claim determined by his success.   Sometimes there is a teacher's class — a class from which the
teachers for the inferior classes are taken, and to which,
having performed their routine of duty, they return; and
with which, during their temporary absence, they are
enabled to keep pace, by private and occasional study,
(some of the least necessary tasks being meanwhile dispensed with,) and by the advantages derived from the
act of teaching.   Such varieties may often occur under
able preceptors, in strict conformity with the System of
Mutual Tuition.   It is only those, who are unacquainted
with its principle, or fail in practice, that look upon such
variations in its application, as changes in the System.

In general, however, an able master will prize an able
teacher, and find means of retaining him as long as is
fitting.   Frequent changes are inconvenient, and should
not be made without good reason.

Having now treated on the *scheme, the general laws,*

and regulations, for the administration of the universal principle of Mutual Instruction and moral Discipline—all that properly constitutes the Madras System of Education—we come to the application of this system to the different branches of study in a course of elementary education, limited, in general, to the National Schools.

PART III.

On the Practices of the Madras School; or the Methods pursued in the Application of Mutual Tuition to a Course of Elementary Education.

CHAP. I.—*On the Course of Study.*

§ 1. " *Begin always with those things which are best known, and most obvious; whereby the mind may have no difficulty or fatigue, and proceed by regular and easy steps, to things that are most difficult. And, as far as possible, let not the understanding, or the proof of any of our positions depend on the positions that follow, but always on those which go before.*"—WATTS.

" Not only in the instruction of a school, but in all instruction, in every art and science, the primary rule, which ought never to be lost sight of, is, that the scholar read with understanding, and be made intimately acquainted, nay, habitually familiar with every lesson as he goes along.

" This rule goes to the foundation of all instruction. So essential is it, that you may almost pronounce on the merit of any school by the grounding, as it is called, of the scholar well; and of every system of education, by the facility, satisfaction, and despatch with which it enables the master to communicate and ensure, and the scholar to acquire and retain, *perfect instruction.*

" The first care, therefore, of a master of a Madras School, or any school, or of a parent or tutor, should be, to prepare a course of studies, duly arranged, in a methodical series, gradually and almost imperceptibly progressive, ' *a notioribus adminus nota;*' so that each lesson may be intimately connected with that which went before, and that which follows after it. This process has its foundation in human nature, belongs to every art and science, as well as to literature, and has been inculcated by the most eminent writers of every age."—*Ludus Literarius*, pp. 97—99.

" Young pupils require to be put into the road, and this road ought to be plain, accessible, and free from intricacy."—QUIN.

"In the course of studies, therefore, prepared for the use of schools, all complication must be avoided: each part should be of a just length, sufficient for the complete instruction and exercise of the scholar in that branch; and, at the same time, should contain nothing but what is absolutely requisite for this purpose. This is what has been attempted to be done in the order of books lately prepared for the schools of the National Society."—*Ludus Literarius*, p. 102.

§ 2. *Prospectus of the practices of the Madras School.*

The System of Mutual Tuition, with perfect instruction, by short, continued, and adapted lessons, and in classes, composed of scholars of equal proficiency, is now to be applied to the several stages of the scholar's progress through an English school.

At Madras, the Author did not content himself with having developed a new and powerful *organ* for the most expeditious, pleasant, and economical mode of conducting education in general, for preventing idleness and offences, and superseding corporeal and other debasing punishments, by constant inspection and vigilance—by incessant occupation—by the power of imitation—the love of activity—the thirst for knowledge—and by the *incitement of emulation*, and a sense of honour and shame; and with having devised the most ready and efficacious guides and checks, by which the execution of this system might be directed, superintended, controlled, and ensured, as has been above detailed;—but he also descended to every particular step in the scholar's progress, and contrived certain practices or methods, to facilitate and expedite each individual operation. His design was always one, simplicity, ease, effect. The measures, which he all along contrived, were solely such as seemed to him naturally conducive to those purposes, and the uniform test of those measures was *experience.* Every process of the New School rests its firm footing on the basis of numerous facts, and repeated experiments. On this ground, the Author has, in the course of his experience at home, made some additions to the subordinate practices of the Madras Asylum in the schools of the National Society, all of them flowing directly from the principles there laid down; and consisting in reducing them to their utmost simplicity, and carrying them to their full extent.

The following brief summary of the Madras practices, as they exist in the Central and other well-conducted Schools of the National Society, will enable the reader to form an idea of the present state of these schools, and prepare him for entering more readily into the spirit of the subsequent instructions.

1. The school opens and closes every day with prayers read or repeated by one of the scholars; and a grace before meat is said, at the breaking up of the morning school.

2. The instruction is carried on by writing and reading at the same time. Every initiatory lesson is taught, by copying it from book before it is learned, and by writing it, as it is spelt off book, after it has been learned. At first, the written characters only are taught, and so taught, that the printed are afterwards learned insensibly.

3. The child is simultaneously taught the alphabet, to write, and to spell on and off book, by a uniform series of lessons; such, that a few examples enable him, by the exercise of his little mind in which he delights, to dictate for himself the succeeding lessons.

4. He learns monosyllables, by spelling them on and off book, and polysyllables by syllabic reading, and unreiterated spelling.

5. The fifth practice of the National School is, that of each child pronouncing to himself, in a low tone of voice, whatever is said or read by his class-fellows — a practice which cannot fail to keep up the attention of every member of the class, at every instant of time, when reading, as was before done by writing, the lesson. It secures also the slow and distinct enunciation of each in turn, and carries the power of imitation to its full length.

6. The sixth practice must be peculiarly interesting to all who are well versed in the Madras System, as it carries, what alone remained to be done, the method of resolving every sentence in reading into its elementary parts. In the initiatory lessons, each child in turn reads

a single *pause*, that is, the smallest portion of a sentence, which conveys a *distinct idea*. Each child is thus, at once, taught to reduce every sentence into its component parts, which, by fixing the eye, the voice, and the mind, on a single idea, or object, tends at once to the utmost distinctness in reading, and the perfect understanding of what is read, and keeps the whole class alive by the brisk circulation. Thus is the grand spring or principle of the Madras System—the tuition by the scholars themselves, actually carried to its utmost limits. Every child becomes his own teacher, and determines, by his own reason, how much it is proper for him to read, and is habitually instructed to analyse for himself the sense of what he reads, pausing at, and digesting, every idea, as he proceeds.

In like manner, and for the same reason, when the child is further advanced, he reads by *clauses*, consisting of *one or more pauses*. These larger portions, which it is proper for him to read, he determines by the breaks in the sense, and according to the progress and size of the class, but so as always to keep up a brisk circulation. The mechanical practice of stopping only at the end of points, requires no mind, and does not exercise the understanding.

7. The seventh practice of the National School is of the same description: when the lesson has been read, the members of the class, in succession, question one another on its meaning. Here each child is tutor and pupil in turn, and the incitement of emulation operates as well in the art of questioning as answering: The teacher and assistant act as umpires; seeing that no fit questions are omitted, and no unfitting ones asked; and correcting, if necessary, the answers when the scholars fail. What may not have been understood when read, is made palpable to every comprehension. By these means all the children are qualified to become teachers, by being habitually practised in the highest duty, in point of instruction, belonging to that character; and a lasting foundation is laid for their invariable attention to the sense of all they read, not only as scholars, but, what is far more, as teachers. The grand object of the

Madras System, and of the National Society, in adopting it — to instil into the infant mind the principles of genuine Christianity; to make them understand, as well as read, their Bibles,—is greatly promoted by the habits of accuracy, to which the practices, here alluded to, especially conduce.

We are now prepared to proceed to details of the practices, of which we have seen the heads.

CHAP. II.—*On Writing and Transcribing.*

" The art of writing a good current hand, which was wont to be so generally neglected by gentlemen, is of no small concern."—QUIN.

In the Madras System of Education, as practised in the Central, and other well-conducted schools of the National Society, every initiatory lesson begins and ends with *writing it.* It is convenient, therefore, to commence the *instructions* for conducting these lessons with some observations on *this practice.*

The art of writing is rendered entirely subservient to the art of reading; or rather, writing and reading go hand in hand, and are mutually auxiliary, the one to the other. In the elementary part of the course, every lesson in reading is a copy in writing, and every copy in writing is a lesson in reading—a practice which excites interest, begets attention, and prevents idleness.

By this process, an art, which, when, as is generally the case, it is solely confined to the mechanical use of the pen, has occupied so large a portion of the learner's time at an advanced period, and keeps the mind locked up, when it can be so profitably employed, may, in the new school, be truly said to be acquired, at an early age, in less than no time. For, while the transcribing of every lesson gradually initiates the scholar into a current hand, and, by continual practice, and unceasing emulation, produces early proficiency, it forwards and perfects him in his reading lessons*, which are thereby sooner acquired;

---

* A single fact will correct a common mistake as to the time in which lessons are written. The monosyllabic book, which, in many schools, has occupied three or four months in the perusal, has been

G

so that the time requisite for learning to write, is actually a negative quantity—less than nothing.

The classes of a school, while supposed to be preparing their lessons, at their seats, or even in reading them, in the usual manner, on the floor, often make little or no progress, the time being lost by imperfect instruction, or wasted in idleness; but in writing, however carelessly executed, something is done, or, at least, it is visible and known whether it be done or not.

In the prosecution of this plan, the Central School of the National Society, availing itself of the recent invention of *stereotype* and *lithography*, have printed, in a large current hand, a script card *of the alphabets, stops and points, and digits,* which serves the scholar as a *perpetual prototype* for writing, when he has no other copy-head; and likewise eight leaves of initiatory lessons in *spelling, writing,* and *reading,* which is called the script or first book. The scholar is also furnished with a small slate, (which is suspended about the neck, or otherwise,) so as to be always at hand for use.

With this preparation, two able, expert, and trusty boys, are selected as teacher and assistant to the class of beginners, and a tutor from a superior class is assigned to each child for a few days, till he has acquired sufficient use of his eyes and fingers to copy letters and figures without such help.

The tutors begin with instructing their pupils to copy the lessons of the same size, form, and distance of letters and lines as the prototype, and without ruling, which serves only to prevent the scholar from learning to write straight—an art which, when not taught in the commencement, is seldom, if ever, acquired without much practice after leaving school.

At first, the tutors guide, if necessary, the fingers of their pupils over the copy, and next on the slate, at once teaching them to incline every letter to the left. At the same time they may instruct them to mark the beginning and ending of each line with the pencil, by measuring (for a few days only) the distance from the top

transcribed by boys, who have made some progress, in as many hours : and may be transcribed by a good writer in one hour.

or bottom of the slate, or by applying to it the prototype, or by a slip of paper, or otherwise. The lines, like those of the copy, should be three-tenths or nearly one-third of an inch apart, the body of the letters being two-thirds of that distance, so that slates seven inches long will contain about eighteen lines, and others in proportion. The reason of writing so close is, that the inspection on the part of the master or visitor, may be less frequently necessary, and less liable to be neglected. No apprehension need be entertained about the scholars not writing wide when allowed.

When the superior tutors are dispensed with, the class is paired off at their seats into tutors and pupils, the superior members tutoring the inferior.

Let the master take especial care that the learners always make due use of their prototype, and that their places be invariably assigned according to their performance*, or approximation to their copy, and their improvement will be uniformly progressive, till, in no long time, they can nearly make a *fac-simile* of it; after which, they are advanced, as a reward of their proficiency, to write with pen and ink. They should immediately learn to make their pens for themselves.

For holding the pen (and even the pencil, which is sometimes put into a case of tin, or a quill,) the following brief rules must here suffice,—

" *I maintain that every man who has the use of his eyes and right-hand, may write what hand he pleases, consequently a good one.*"— CHESTERFIELD.

" 1st, Sit at a convenient distance from the table;—2d, Let the body rest principally on the left arm;—3d, Rest the right arm slightly on the edge of the table, between the wrist and the elbows;—4th, Keep the right arm near your side;—5th, Let the hand rest on the little finger, having the one next to it bent a little inwards;—6th, Hold the pen loosely;—7th, Let the top of the pen point to the right shoulder;—8th, Keep the point of the thumb opposite the first joint of the fore finger;—9th, The point of the pen to be nearly an inch from the end of the finger."—ERWIN.

* At the same time the utmost despatch must be used in the inspection of their writing. A single glance of the eye suffices for each slate. Any unintentional or slight mistakes, in assigning places, will balance themselves at the end of the week or month.

At school, a great deal of unnecessary time is wasted in writing text and half-text, and such hands as are of very infrequent use, to the neglect of that *current hand,* which is of continual use, and which, when acquired, enables the scholar, without previous practice, to write these large hands. It is lamentable to think how many of the precious hours of childhood have hitherto been wasted in learning to write from copy-heads, which have little or no tendency to advance the course of the scholar's studies, contribute to his amusement, or add to his stock of knowledge; a proof of itself that the science of education is yet in its infancy.

The child, having acquired a largish current hand, can readily learn to write in any hand that may be required; provided the lessons, which are given him to transcribe, be written, or *script,* in that hand.

In academies, and large schools, by the separation of the writing and reading departments,* an additional master is required, additional expense incurred, and the advantages of forwarding the elementary lessons by copying them, and of early practice and early habits, are entirely lost; whereby the acquisition of a good current hand is always retarded, and often prevented.

It is a beneficial practice, at the weekly examinations, that the copy and ciphering-books of the advanced classes, and the slates of the rest of the school, (the slates being previously filled with a lesson in writing on one side, and a sum in arithmetic on the other), be arranged, in order of the performance, on the desks, or benches, each child putting his name on his slate or copy. This practice deserves particular notice. It affords, at once, the readiest mode of inspection to the master as well as the visitors, occupying only a few minutes in the largest school; and, on the part of the scholars, produces no small exertion to obtain precedence.

After the inspection of each slate, the owner may be required, if thought necessary, to write off hand, for five or ten minutes, a specimen, to ascertain that there has been no collusion.

---

* The same observation applies to the ciphering department.

If the practice of writing what is to be learned were to be followed up in the advanced lessons, it would also contribute not a little to the art of thinking. The impression on the mind of *once writing* a lesson or book, for the purpose of learning and study, is said to be equal to that of merely reading it *five or six* times.

Before the invention of printing, when books were scarce and dear, it was usual for the student to transcribe a book for his own use, and, by so doing, to make the production of the author, as it were, his own. Demosthenes is said to have transcribed Thucydides eight times. Though it is not proposed to continue the practice of copying books (since the chief reasons for its continuance have ceased), farther than the initiatory tracts, which can be written, as well as read, in less time than is generally employed solely in reading them; yet it may be advisable for the student to make a summary of such compositions, as are worth the while; by which the understanding will be exercised, and the subject imprinted on the mind, at an age that is susceptible of the deepest and most lasting impression.

For the richer classes of society, abstracts, or epitomes, of treatises on morality and religion, and of the sciences (such as arithmetic, grammar, geography, algebra, &c.), containing first elements, and general principles, should be composed and published in *script*, as will undoubtedly be the case before the end of the century. Such, if properly executed, and adapted to the ready comprehension and consequent amusement of the infant mind, may be entirely transcribed and perused with great advantage.

In a word, to copy the elementary lessons on slate, and the more-advanced lessons on paper, is the easiest, surest, and most expeditious method of instruction in reading and learning, as well as, writing. It requires, as far as the writing is concerned, neither ability in the master, nor capacity in the scholar. Nothing more is requisite, to ensure that every scholar (like an engraver) make a fac-simile of his prototype, than uniform and unceasing attention to the few general rules which have been laid down. Indeed, the printed characters might be entirely superseded, if *script* books were made general.

It would be inexcusable to conclude this Chapter without entreating the attention of parents to the manifest advantages of simultaneous instruction in the elements of letters and the art of writing; and to the necessity of firmness and perseverance with young children in the commencement. In the first lessons alone, can any obstacle occur, owing to the natural difficulty of a new task, to the want of expert tutors, and of the imitation and emulation of a Madras School, and to the prejudice and reluctance of those about them. But if the parent, who has naturally and generally the charge of the infant mind, can remove these obstacles, the reward is certain, in the early gratification and improvement of the child, and the ease and satisfaction with which his subsequent lessons can be carried on.—*See Essay on Domestic Education*, LUDUS LITERARIUS, p. 189.

CHAP. III.— *On simultaneous Instruction in Reading and Writing.*

"Quapropter id non mediocriter conducet, si scribere ab initio didicerint, et in eo se vehementer exercuerint, quod etiam ad legendi expeditionem non parum conferet." *—Baptista Quarinus.*

Before proceeding, it is recommended to the master to read the first section of the Chapter on Morality and Religion, in which he will find directions for teaching the *viva voce lessons* with which every child begins, on his admission to school. He may then read the former part of the Chapter on Arithmetic, for a practical elucidation of the methodical and progressive order in which every branch of education ought to be conducted. .

§ 1. *Introductory Remarks on distinct and audible Pronunciation.*

In the first instance it may be recommended to parents to pay particular attention* to the just pronunciation of the letters, as soon as the child can articulate, beginning with the vowels. This is the best method of teaching children to speak; and would, in time, put an end to provincial dialect, if sufficient pains were taken, both at home and at school, especially in the preliminary

* The maternal and domestic education of early infancy in Greece and at Rome, furnishes memorable exemplars.

lessons, to correct a vitious pronunciation and habits, before they take root, and become difficult to eradicate.

It is most important to accustom the child at once to read and speak *audibly, distinctly,* and *slowly,* pronouncing aloud the last letter of every syllable, the last syllable of every word, and the last word of every sentence. From the common neglect of this useful rule, it is deplorable to witness the perpetual and intolerable interruption, the loss of time, the indistinctness, and annoyance which are occasioned.

The difficulty often found in teaching children to speak aloud is at once conquered by a process, which, at the same time, forms a good introduction to the elementary lessons, by the teachers practising the whole class in what is called a bawling lesson. They all bawl together ba, be, bi, bo, bu; and also, a, e, i, o, u, ha, he, hi, ho, hu, taking places according to the loudness and right pronunciation of the aspirate. The teacher leads at first, and then each child in succession, till they can all speak aloud. They then learn to modulate their voices to such a pitch, as to be heard distinctly, at their daily lessons, by their teachers and class-fellows; and so much louder at examinations, as to be audible to the visitors, and all around: and at all times thereafter, while each member of a class, in succession, reads or rehearses a portion of the daily lessons, or tasks, the rest repeat along with him in the same tone; at first, till the habit is acquired, in a loud, but after a little practice in a low, voice, so that the repetition may be almost lost in the voice of the speaker, or reader, or scarcely audible; at any rate, so as not to add sensibly to the necessary noise of the rehearsals.

§ 2. *Writing on Sand.*

" *Jesus stooped down, and with his finger wrote on the ground.*"— John viii. 6.

The easiest mode of teaching the letters, digits, points, monosyllables, &c., is by writing them on sand with the finger, which is the simplest, and most manageable instrument. This practice is the only branch of the New School which, as before stated, the Author borrowed from India; and it is the only one which his experience, in the generality of our schools, constituted as they arc, has induced him to relinquish. Owing to the difficulty of superintendence, where the lesson must be effaced as soon as written, and to the consequent neglect, and slow progress, at the sand board, this practice is now, for the most part, superseded by that which was wont to follow: viz.

§ 3. *Writing the Alphabet, and Syllables of Two Letters, on Slate.*

1. By beginning with slate and pencil, and the written characters, a stage of the course is saved; the copying of the printed alphabet, which is of far greater difficulty, and of little or no use, is rendered unnecessary; and the knowledge of the printed characters, as will be seen hereafter, is attained almost insensibly. At the same time, the art of sand-writing, and of reading without writing*, will be sufficiently apparent from the following details of slate-writing—a process which has this manifest advantage, that the lessons remain for inspection till one or both sides of the slate are filled, and shown to the master, so that they can hardly be evaded, or neglected, as at the sand-board, without detection.

2. To teach the alphabet, as it is the first, so it is also the most difficult and irksome task that occurs in the art of tuition, there being no simpler elements to which the letters can be reduced, and no natural connexion between them; nothing that can excite interest, keep up attention, or assist the memory. And though, till this is accomplished, together with the subsequent lessons, in the junction of vowels and consonants, no good progress can be made, and the child can have no satisfaction in his studies; yet it is generally, if not always, the most neglected part of the whole course.

With a view to obviate this difficulty, and to prevent this neglect, the child learns the alphabets and initiatory lessons, by copying them, so as to imprint them on his memory; and this is done by a process that engages his mind, by the suitable exercise which it gives to him, in dictating his successive lessons for himself.

---

* It is only required, in the one case, to substitute *sand* for *slate*; and, in the other, *omit writing* altogether.

In teaching these lessons, the process is the same as described in the *Chapter on Writing.*

3. The first three pages of the script cards, or book, No. 1, contains the letters i, l, t, o, (with which it begins, on account of the simplicity of these characters, consisting of straight lines and a curve, which comprise the elementary forms of most of the alphabet); the vowels, a, e, i, o, u, y; a series formed by the combination of every consonant, in order, with every vowel, beginning with ba, be, bi, bo, bu, and ending with za, ze, zi, zo, zu; and again, of every vowel with every consonant, from ab, eb, ib, ob, ub, to az, ez, iz, oz, uz.

The course of instruction commences (see p. 82, supra) with the appointment of an able, active, expert, and trusty teacher and assistant to the class of beginners, and a tutor from a higher class to each child; or perhaps better, by uniting this class to that which has just learned the initiatory lessons, (see p. 61, supra).

All being seated at the desk, or on the bench, but the teacher and assistant who overlook and direct them, the tutors instruct their pupils to trace, and, as they trace, pronounce the letters i, l, t, o, one by one, over the script primer, and then to copy them on their slates.*

The tutors next teach their pupils to write and name the vowels, one by one, annexing each, as soon as they can make it, to the letter l, as in the card before them,—pointing with the pencil, and pronouncing, by *previous* spelling, or spelling *on book*, as they proceed, l, a, la, l, e, le, l, i, li, l, o, lo, l, u, lu; then reading la, le, &c.; y is omitted for the present, to prevent the confusion of li and ly, and to shorten the first lessons.

When the pupil can execute this task with ease and readiness, his tutor calls upon him to spell and write, on the reverse or back of the slate, each syllable (or word) promiscuously, or in any order that he dictates. The tutor says le, pupil repeats le; then writes and pronounces l, e, le, and so with the rest, la, lo, lu, li. He

---

* By way of practice, the form of the same letter should be copied twenty (always exacting ten) times in a minute; or 200 (never less than 100) times in ten minutes.

then reads them on the slate, as thus written—a practice
which ascertains that the lesson. has not been said by
rote, but is actually known and understood.

. This, too, being properly done, all the members of
the class dispensing, for the present, with the superior
tutors, are arranged on the floor according to their
writing, and go through the same process, both on the
front and back of the slates, in rehearsing or saying this
lesson conjointly to their teachers in the class, as they
before did individually to their tutors, in learning it at
the desk—with this difference, that each, in turn, now
takes only a single letter or syllable (or word); and, for
the sake of distinctness, at the outset, drops the hand at
the end of each letter, as it is written—a practice which
is discontinued, as soon as the habit of steadiness and
regularity is acquired.

Here let the master observe, that it behoves him to
exercise his utmost energy and ingenuity in contriving to
instruct his pupils in the most expeditious, for that is the
best way, to write, spell, and read, in any order, and with
perfect readiness, this primary and model lesson, *la, le,
li, lo, lu;* for this is the key to the subsequent lessons of—

4. *The series formed by the union of consonants and
vowels in order.*

The key, of which the child has just been put in
possession, enables him, by the exercise of his little
mind, in which he delights, to dictate for himself the
series of consonants and vowels, beginning with ba, be,
bi, bo, bu, and ending with za, ze, zi, zo, zu.* All
that is here requisite is, to instruct him to write and
name each consonant in order, and to annex to it the
vowels, as was done with l, proceeding with every successive line, at the desks or seats, and on the floor, as
with the sample which has been given.

Arrived at the end of this first series, ba to zu, the
scholar being now acquainted with all the small alphabet,

---

* The lines beginning with c and g, may, on account of the hard
and soft sounds of these letters, be deferred to the end of the series,
when a few examples with the letter y may be introduced, as ca, ce,
go, gi, ly, by, cy, dy, gy, fy.

may learn the capital -alphabet, either as the letters
occur in his lessons, or by copying one every morning
and evening, in order. The class now proceed to—

5. *A second series of the union of the vowels and
consonants in order.*

This series of lessons commences with a, b, ab,
e, b, eb, i, b, ib, o, b, ob, u, b, ub, and ends with
az, ez, iz, oz, uz.

The only difficulty here lies (as all the letters are now
familiar) in distinguishing the short sound of the vowels,
particularly e and i. Especial pains must, therefore, be
taken with the first line, the key to the rest, which should
be dwelt upon till the learner can perfectly distinguish
these sounds: after which, he has a pleasure in dictating for
himself, according to the example which has been given,
the rest of the series, ac, ec, ic, oc, uc, to az, ez, iz, oz,
uz,* with which these lessons terminate.

Before concluding this chapter, it may be important to
draw the particular attention of the master to these
combinations of vowels and consonants, by remarking,
that one or more of them occurs in every word, except
those of one letter, viz. a, i, o.

Here it may be also observed, that, in learning the lessons, the general rule is that the scholars sit and stand
alternately; but it is no unusual practice to continue
them on the floor for hours together. Seneca says,
that the Roman youth were always on their legs, and
never learned any thing in a sitting posture. And Lord
Bacon says, "that the much sitting of children at school,
hinders their growth:" and experience seems to evince
that the standing and taking of places is a wholesome
exercise. Hence the standing, in writing, at desks of
counting and banking-houses, and by students of me-
dicine, &c.

---

* In teaching the alphabet, as commonly practised at home, with
counters, the vowels and consonants being kept apart, the children,
who do not write, may be taught to pick them up, and place them by
the side of one another, so as to form, spell, and read every syllable
of two letters in the order and manner above described, writing only
excepted.

It should have been before noticed, that the child ought to be taught, in the beginning, to write, name, and know the value of, the stops and points.

CHAP. IV.— *On monosyllabic Reading.*

§ 1. *On the reason of omitting spelling lessons composed of unconnected monosyllables and polysyllables.*

Hitherto the child has had the satisfaction of exercising his mind in forming regular serieses of all the syllables of two letters in the English Language; and has thereby acquired the first rudiments of spelling and reading. On this foundation he has now to rear the fabric of his future studies. From this time his higher faculties are called into immediate and perpetual activity. The tables of monosyllables and polysyllables, with which spelling-books were wont to abound — tables composed of words increasing in difficulty, and like the letters of the Alphabet, having no connexion, and conveying no instruction or amusement, to excite interest, keep up attention, or assist the memory; all such unmeaning and tiresome tasks — are discarded, and the scholar's future exercises in writing, spelling, and reading, are composed of a progressive course of lessons, moral, religious, instructive, and entertaining, all of them, except a few stories in the first part of the second book, extracted or abridged from the Bible. Besides the useful knowledge with which these lessons are fitted to store the mind, they are much easier to be learned and remembered, from the frequent recurrence of the same words, and from the sense of the text and context.

Introductory to this branch of the scholastic course, is the fourth page of the Script cards, consisting of easy lessons of short monosyllables; but it is needless to take particular notice of this page, because it might be erased, if the beginning of the second book was simplified, and because it is written, spelt, and read, as in the subsequent pages. These pages (5—16) are extracted. from the first part of the second book. In them, as before, the copy is the lesson, and the lesson is the copy; so that the scholar has not to look off his book for the prototype of his writing.

These lessons are taught *by writing, by spelling on and off book, by reading by pauses and clauses, and by an examination on the meaning of what is read.* See Summary of Practices, pp. 79, 80.

The spelling has been exemplified in the combination of vowels and consonants. The reading by pauses and clauses, fall to be explained in this chapter. The manner of examination will be noticed here, and more particularly described in the Chapter on Morality and Religion.

§ 2. *On pauses and clauses.*

The scholar, who has been perfectly instructed in the daily rehearsal of the Lord's Prayer, Collects, &c. from the mouth of the teacher, is already accustomed to the subdivisions and divisions of sentences and lessons, by pauses and clauses.

An observation of Quintilian will serve to illustrate the use of pauses. *The difficulty* (he says) *of learning to read is, that, while with the voice we are pronouncing one part of a sentence, with our eyes we are looking forward to another.* To this may be added, that, at the same time, we are gathering the meaning of the whole sentence in our mind.

Now, in the National Schools, an attempt has been made, with good success, to obviate this difficulty; and, as has been said before, to *fix the eye, the voice, and the mind,* on a single object in succession, by the subdivision of the lesson into pauses, which not only conduces greatly to correct reading, but also to the understanding of what is read. The combining of two or more ideas, puzzles and perplexes children; for which, the best remedy is, to accustom them to distinguish, by an intermission in reading, and to dwell on, each of the minutest subdivisions in the sense.

Another advantage of pause-reading in the initiatory and short lessons is, that, by the quick succession, it distributes a minute portion of the lesson to each member of the class, without reading it over oftener than is necessary to learn it. Besides which, it is the best introduction to reading by clauses.

When the scholars have made some progress, or when they revise what they have before read by pauses, and

H

the lessons are lengthened, they read them by clauses, or
such proportions, according to the breaks in the sense, as
may keep up a brisk circulation.   Duly to apportion the
length of each clause, requires perpetual attention to the
thread of the discourse; whereas, always stopping at a
period, or given point, is only a servile exercise of the
eye, and may be done without paying any regard to the
sense, or understanding a word that is read.

§ 3. *Now to return to the monosyllabic lessons of the
script cards.*

The method of learning these lessons being the same
with that which has been exemplified in the last chapter,
in the combinations of vowels and consonants, with the
addition only of reading by pauses and clauses, an example
will suffice in this place.

The lessons begin at the fifth page.   The (figure) 5 is
written on the right-hand corner of the slate, at the top,
and forms a detached task, not to interfere with the
regular lessons.   The pupil then copies and learns the
first lesson, 1, by previous spelling (on book)—2, by
words, 3, by pauses, 4, by spelling the hard words off
book, and 5, by examining on the sense; thus,

1. By previous spelling, T, h, e, the; w, a, y, way; o,
f, of; G, o, d, God; i, s, is; a, a; g, oo, d, good; w,
a, y, way. The lesson, thus written and spelt, is read by
previous spelling, as often (but no oftener) as is necessary, to
enable the scholar to read it without resolving the word into
letters.*

2. It is then read by words, thus:—The, way, of, God, is, a,
good, way,—till the scholars can read it readily.

3. It is read by pauses, thus: The way—of God—is—a good
way,—till the scholars can read it well.

4. They then spell the hard words off book, writing on the
back of the slate each letter, as it is pronounced.   Thus, teacher
says *way*, pupil repeats *way*, and writes and spells w, a, y,
way.—T. good—P. good; g, oo, d, good.—T. the—P. the;
t, h, e, the.

5. Lastly, they are examined on the meaning, thus:—
Question. What is the way of God?—Answer. A good way.—

* If this lesson be found too long, it may be divided into five.
1 The way, 2 of God, 3 is, 4 a good way. 5 The way—of God—is—
a good way.

Q. What is a good way?—A. The way of God.—Q. Whose way is a good way?—A. God's.*

In like manner, they proceed throughout the script book, the lessons gradually advancing in length.

At the end of the sections, which are marked lessons, 1, 2, 3, &c., each is revised, by reading it over in one or more lessons; and, at the end of this book, the whole is revised by sections, or in eight lessons.

Not to interrupt the thread of these processes, they have been stated by themselves. The question now is, *by whom* are these lessons taught? This must be left to the discretion of the master, who will be determined by the age or capacity of the scholars.

If the class, being paired off into tutors and pupils, can readily proceed, under the direction and instruction of their teachers, they do so accordingly. But if they cannot, the aid of superior tutors must, in the beginning, be called in, as before, in the union of vowels and consonants; and each pupil reads and says, in the manner that has been described, the whole lesson to his tutor. The class then go to their places on the floor, and repeat the same lesson in all its stages to the teachers, as before individually to their tutors; only with this difference, that now each scholar, in succession, takes a single letter, or word, or pause, as it falls.

The child named, or pointed to, whom, and those next in order, we call 1, 2, 3, &c., each in succession writes, spells, and pronounces distinctly, what falls to him; the rest of the class writing and repeating after, or almost with, him, in a low voice, hardly audible. The above example, repeated, for the sake of distinctness, and marked as it is now to be read, will stand thus:

1 T, 2 h, 3 e; 4 The, 5 w, 6 a, 7 y, 8 way, 9 o, 10 f, 11 of, 12 G, 13 o, 14 d, 15 God, 16 i, 17 s, 18 is, 19 a, 20 a, 21 g, 22 oo, 23 d, 24 good, 25 w, 26 a, 27 y, 28 way.

---

* The sentence is not well chosen to begin with; for we can hardly propose the question, What does the word *way* mean? or enter on an exposition of it here, as, e. g. The way of God means the doings of God, or what God does; or the course of his providence and dealings with men. Indeed, in the whole of the preparatory tracts, care must be taken to adapt the questions and the explanations to the capacity of the children.

The lesson thus written and spelt on book, is read by words, calling the next in order 1, 2, 3, &c.

1 The, 2 way, 3 of, 4 God, 5 is, 6 a, 7 good, 8 way.

Lastly, it is read by pauses.

1 The way—2 of God—3 is—4 a good way.

The directions for spelling off book, for the examination on the sense, and for the revisals, need not, be repeated here.

§ 4. *On teaching the printed characters.*

The script cards finished, the class proceed to the second book, from the beginning of which the lessons, they have just learned, were transcribed. They now read the same lessons in this printed book. From their previous knowledge of them, and the similarity of the printed and written characters, they insensibly acquire the former, while they still further perfect themselves in these initiatory lessons. These lessons are best learned, by transcribing the printed into written characters, for which, and every future lesson, their sole copy-head is the *prototype script card.*

Having revised these lessons, till they can readily read them in the printed book, they go through the remainder of the monosyllabic part of this book, writing, reading, and spelling, &c., as before.

Finally, they may once more revise the whole thirteen pages, in a single lesson.

In concluding this chapter, it may not be quite useless again to notice, that these thirteen pages can be read, distinctly and deliberately, in thirteen minutes, or about a quarter of an hour; and that they can be transcribed, by a fast writer, in an hour. It seldom, however, happens that the scholars spend less than three or four months, and frequently three or four times as long, in solely learning to read them. Such is the consequence, when the master, forgetful of his duty, does not take the trouble to direct and superintend his ministers in such a manner, that every day, and every hour, may be marked by a competent share of progress.

CHAP. V.—*On promiscuous Reading-lessons.*

With the former part of the Second Book, ends monosyllabic reading by previous spelling; but if a monosyllable occur, in the course of the future lessons, which the scholar cannot read at once, he spells *on book* that word, and that only; and this is best done by running over the letters silently in his mind. He now proceeds to the last stage in the art of reading, which consists of promiscuous lessons, composed of *monosyllables and polysyllables.**

The child is initiated into this branch of his study, not, as has been observed, by tedious and unprofitable tables (or columns) of unconnected and unmeaning words; but by the same lessons, whereby his moral and religious instruction is carried on.

1. It is necessary to begin with a brief explanation of the practices of syllabic reading, and unreiterated spelling, by which the child is instructed in reading and spelling the polysyllables, as they occur.

As monosyllables were taught by *previous spelling*, resolving them into the letters of which they were composed: so *polysyllables* are taught, as they occur in the daily lessons, by *syllabic reading;* that is, resolving them into the syllables of which they are composed, in order to their re-union into one articulation — a practice by which every word, however long, is converted, as it were, into monosyllables: thus,

Pre-sent, present; re-pre-sent, represent; mis-re-pre-sent-a-ti-on, misrepresentation.
The advantage, as well in point of principle, as of time, is obvious, and sanctioned by the experience of more than thirty years.

The art of reading monosyllables having been before acquired, the resolution of the separate syllables into letters, by *previous spelling*, is unnecessary; and the repetitions, in doing so, are both superfluous and tiresome. As, for example, the old school spells,

M, i, s, mis, r, e, re, misre, p, r, e, pre, misrepre, s, e, n, t, sent, misrepresent, a, a, misrepresenta, t, i, ti, misrepresentati, o, n, on, misrepresentation.†

---

* For the sake of brevity, I denote a word of two or more syllables by the term *polysyllable*, whether dissyllable, trisyllable, or polysyllable properly so called.

† That such practices should have been continued to the present age, can only be attributed to the effect of ancient usage, inveterate habits,

H 3

This process is simplified and abridged in the Madras School, as just stated, by *syllabic reading;* thus,

Mis-re-pre-sent-a-ti-on, misrepresentation.

Again, in spelling *off book*, after the lesson has been read, there are, in the old school, throughout the whole course, nay, it may be said, through life, the same weari-some and superfluous reiterations, which have been seen in spelling *on book*,

M, i, s, mis, r, e re, misre, &c.

In the Madras School, this process of spelling off book has also been simplified and abbreviated by *unreiterated spelling.* The word being first, for the sake of distinct-ness, pronounced syllabically,

Mis-re-pre-sent-a-ti-on, is spelt simply and shortly thus: m, i, s—r, e—p, r, e—s, e, u, t—a—t, i—o, n.

In calling upon the class to spell, after the lesson has been said, it should be noticed that the longest words are not always the most difficult; but those in which some of the letters are silent, or cannot be distinguished by the pronunciation, such as,

Tongue, phlegm, beauty, wrought, height, leave, receive, believe, &c.

And on account of the aspirate,

At, hat; eat, heat; ill, hill; arbour, harbour; witch, which, &c.

2. Thus prepared, the scholar enters on the reading lessons, consisting of monosyllables and polysyllables indiscriminately.

This branch of the course commences with the inter-esting History of *Joseph and his Brethren*, in four parts, which together form the second part of the second book. The manner of reading this history, and every subsequent book, differs in nothing from what has already been described in the former Chapter, except that, as *there*, the *monosyllables* were, in the first instance, read on book by *previous spelling;* so *here* the *polysyllables* are, in the first instance, read *on book* by *syllabic reading*, and spelt *off book*, after the lesson has been read, by *unreiterated spell-ing.* An example will suffice to illustrate what is meant.

This history begins at p. 14, which is written on the corner of the slate, as before directed.

and antiquated authority—barriers still opposed to the progress of the new System of Education.

The first lesson is the argument or contents, which the children read in order, each taking a pause.

1 The (His-to-ry) History—2 of (Jo-seph) Joseph—3 and— 4 his (Bre-thren) Brethren.

The lesson once read over by syllabic reading, may be read again in the same manner, but no oftener than is requisite to learn to pronounce the *poly-syllables* at once, without resolving them into (mono) syllables; after which it is revised without syllabic reading, till it is duly learned, thus:—

1 The History—2 of Joseph—3 and—4 his Brethren.

After this lesson follows—

Part I.

—which is written by itself, as the number of the page was.

The next and following lessons go on, as just described, thus :

1 Now—2 (Ja-cob) Jacob—3 (lov-ed) loved—4 (Jo-seph*) Joseph—5 more than all his (child-ren) children, and so on.

In like manner, the class proceed throughout the whole of this history, resolving such words, and such only, into syllables, as they cannot otherwise read—the lessons daily growing in length.

Sometimes the polysyllabic words are written and learned before the class begin to read the lesson. But the best way is to write the whole of this book, which brings the scholar fast forward with his reading as well as writing, and may be done in far less time than is generally imagined. All along, after a lesson has been learned and said, the teacher examines the class, or, which is preferable, the scholars are taught to examine one another, on the meaning of every word and member of a sentence, at first with the books open, and afterwards with them shut, each in turn putting the question to the scholar opposite to him; after which the hard words are spelt off book,—the polysyllables by unreiterated spelling.

Next they revise this part of the history, reading it by clauses. They then go through the three other parts in the same manner; and, lastly, they once more revise

---

* Joseph having occurred before, or any other word which can be read without resolving it into syllables, may be so read at once.

the whole four Parts, which, if before perfectly taught,
may be done in four lessons.*

3. *On the perusal of the subsequent Tracts in the Course
     of Instruction in the National Schools.*

These are—1, Our Saviour's Sermon on the Mount—
2, Parables—3, Miracles—4, Discourses—5, History—
and 6, Ostervald's Abridgment of the Bible.

Having now briefly propounded the processes, or
methods of instruction in all the branches of the art of
reading, it will be observed, that the uniform aim has
been *simplification*—the resolution of every thing that is
complex, into its elementary parts—monosyllables into
the letters, and polysyllables into the syllables, of which
they are composed—sentences into the pauses, or the
smallest members which contain a distinct idea—and
lessons into clauses†, or larger portions of the discourse,
according to the breaks in the sense, the progress and
size of the class,—shorter in the beginning, and longer as
the class and lessons advance.

Of these practices, previous spelling ceases, when the
scholars can read monosyllables, without resolving them
into letters: and syllabic-reading, when they can read
the polysyllables, without resolving them into (mono) syllables.   In the perusal, therefore, of the subsequent tracts,
there is no more previous spelling, or syllabic reading, except when words occur which the scholar cannot otherwise
read.   But the reading by clauses, so important to the
understanding, as well as to the circulation of the lessons,
and unreiterated spelling (off book), so material to the
saving of time, are continued throughout the whole course
of study.   Nor should pause-reading be rashly abandoned, till the scholar is perfectly familiar with this practice, which is the best preparative for reading by clauses,
and is attended with peculiar distinctness, and a brisk
circulation of the lesson.   Previously, therefore, to *con-
ning* each of the subsequent lessons by clauses, it may

---

* As in the monosyllabic, so in the polysyllabic, part of this book, a
few easier lessons might be prefixed with advantage. Indeed, the
2d book would admit of considerable improvement, especially for the
higher order of schools.

† See examples below, p. 101—3.

be once, or oftener, if requisite, rehearsed by pauses,
Nor need this practice terminate, but with the above-
mentioned tracts, by which time the scholar ought to be
well versed in the art of reading, and duly prepared for the
perusal of larger treatises, and the study of the Bible in
the manner, which will be treated on, in the next chapter.
· It may be added, that, though the ostensible reading
by pauses ceases when the Bible is taken in hand, yet,
at all times, and on all occasions, a judicious reader
makes a frequent use of pauses, sometimes scarcely
sensible, and sometimes strikingly marked, as may be
noticed in the elocution of the best readers, speakers,
and orators.

Further to illustrate this subject, there may be subjoined—

4. *A few examples, with remarks, on reading by pauses,
and by clauses.*

The following examples are so marked, that they
serve, at once, as specimens of reading by pauses and
by clauses. A pause is a given quantity, being invariably limited to the minutest portion of a sentence,
which contains a meaning. Clauses may be varied with
the breaks in the sense, the length of the lesson, and
the size of the class. They are generally short in the
elementary books, for the sake of a quick circulation,
where the lessons are brief, and lengthened in the revisals,
in proportion to the lesson; but so that a portion may
fall to each member of the class, without repeating
it oftener than is necessary to learn it. Thus, when
the monosyllabic book, of thirteen pages, is revised by a
class of thirty-six scholars, at one reading, a clause may,
on an average, be about one-third or one-sixth of a page,
that each scholar may have one or two clauses, and so in
other cases.

The following examples are taken—1, from the 2d
Book—2, the Sermon on the Mountain—and 3, the
Catechism.

· 1. The 2d Book.

The way—of God—is—a good way. | Bad men—are foes—to
God. |

Again—There is not—a thought—in our hearts—but—God—

knows it. | p. 14. The History—of Joseph—and—his Brethren. |
Part 1. | Now—Jacob—loved—Joseph—more than all his
children, | because—he was—the son—of his old age. |

P. 18. | In the seven plenteous years—the earth—brought forth
abundantly; | and—Joseph—gathered up—all the food—which
was—in the land, | and—laid it up—in the cities. |

2. Sermon on the Mount.

Jesus, — seeing—the multitudes, — went up—into a moun-
tain; | and, when he was set, his disciples—came—unto him, |
and — he opened—his mouth, — and — taught them,— saying,
| Blessed — are — the poor—in spirit, | for—theirs — is — the
kingdom—of heaven. |

3. *In teaching the Catechism,* in order to keep up general attention, by a brisk circulation, each repetition of
the lesson should include as many scholars as may be—
allowing to each a competent portion, according to the
progress of the class. The common practice in the Old
School is, for each boy to rehearse a question, in
succession, the rest listening, or not, as may be; and, in
learning a question at one lesson, each, in turn, rehearses
the whole: whereas, in the initiatory lessons of a Madras
School, each child, in succession, rehearses a single pause,
all the rest repeating with him; so that the following
example, containing eighty-eight pauses, would occupy
as many boys, in rotation; and, in a class of thirty-six
children, would circulate about two and a half times.
The class, when further advanced, repeat this question
by clauses, so that one rehearsal occupies twelve
children, and three include the whole class, and furnish a
specimen of their proficiency; but if the class consists of
twelve scholars, one rehearsal would include the whole
class. The clauses are marked 1, 2, 3, &c.

1 My duty—towards my neighbour, is—to love him—as—
myself, and—to do—to all men, as—I would—they should do—
unto me : 2 To love, honour, and—succour—my father—and—
mother: 3 To honour—and—obey the king, and—all—that are
put—in authority—under him: 4 To submit myself—to all my
governors, teachers, spiritual pastors—and—masters: 5 To
order myself—lowly—and—reverently—to all my betters: 6 To
hurt nobody—by word—nor—deed: 7 To be true—and—
just—in all my dealings: 8 To bear no malice—nor—hatred—
in my heart; 9 To keep—my hands—from picking—and—

stealing, and—my tongue—from evil-speaking, lying, and—slandering: 10 To keep—my body—in temperance, soberness, and—chastity: 11 Not to covet—nor—desire—other men's goods: 12 But—to learn—and—labour—truly—to get—mine own living, and—to do—my duty—in that state—of life,—unto which—it shall please—God—to call me.

It is not necessary to be fastidious about pauses and clauses, wherever there is ground for difference of opinion, or room for an option. Thus, in the first clause, the pause, " *they should do,*" might have been marked, " *they—should do;*" and in the last clause, " *it shall please—God,*" which is thus divided, because it is often advisable to pause, for the sake of reverence, before and after the holy name of God, might have been included in one pause; and the 9th and 12th clauses might each be divided into two clauses.

This subject will be resumed in the next chapter.

CHAP. VI.—*On Morality and Religion.*

" In primis inspici mores opórtebit."—QUINTILIAN.
" Suffer the little children to come unto me, and forbid them not, for of such is the kingdom of God." Mark x. 14.
" If the generous seeds of religion and virtue be not carefully sown in the tender minds of children—and if those seeds be not cultivated by good education, there will certainly spring up briars and thorns, of which parents will not only feel the inconvenience, but every body else that comes near them."—TILLOTSON.

Morality and Religion are the basis of the whole course of study in the National Schools. The elementary books, there taught, are almost entirely taken from the Holy Scriptures, and form a compendious System of Christian Instruction.

All the facilities of the Madras System apply, as well to the first principles of moral and religious instruction, as to writing, and the rudiments of reading and spelling, with which indeed they are, in this manual, inseparably linked together, and under which heads, they have been already in part treated of.

§ 1. *On viva-voce Lessons.*

" The Lord's Prayer, the Creed, and Ten Commandments, he should learn by heart, not by reading them himself in his *primer*, but by somebody's repeating them before he can read."—LOCKE.

It is one of the exercises of the children of a Madras School, from the day of their admission, to repeat, from

the mouth of their teacher, for a quarter of an hour,
morning and evening, a small portion of those prayers
and graces, that are of daily use, beginning with the
Lord's Prayer, which is restored, as it were, to its wonted
place in the horn-book. Then follow graces before and
after meat—the Second and Third Collect of Morning
and Evening Prayer—a short prayer before and after
Divine Service—the Creed—the Decalogue—their Duty
towards God and their Neighbour, &c. The first lessons,
as given by the teacher, are re-echoed in the same voice,
by the whole class, who are at once taught to pronounce
audibly, slowly, and distinctly. Each lesson may consist
of a single pause, or smallest member of a sentence,
containing an idea. Thus, 1st lesson,—Our Father—
2d, which art—3d, in heaven—4th, Our Father—which
art—in heaven. One or more pauses, or the whole clause,
or as much as the class can well learn by heart in a
quarter of an hour, should be perfectly taught the first
morning, and so every succeeding evening and morning.
The former lessons being repeated every day previously
to entering on the subsequent one, the lessons will
gradually lengthen as the scholars advance, and their
minds are more and more opened, for the reception
of progressive instruction, and as the memory improves,
by exercise. It is easy to see how much a very small
portion learnt perfectly by heart, every morning and
evening, will amount to, before the scholar is yet fully
instructed in the art of reading, with the acquisition of
which, however, these *viva-voce* repetitions off book,
must not materially interfere; for it is by his daily lessons
in reading, that religious knowledge is most readily and
effectually attained; therefore the utmost pains must be
taken from the beginning, to forward him in this art,
by which he may the sooner be qualified to read and
learn for himself, on book, the *memoriter* lessons, as
well in exercises at school, as in tasks at home, and
with better understanding, and consequently with greater
profit, than from the mouth of another. Nor are the
primary rehearsals, from the mouth of the teacher, idle in
this respect; they serve to form a just enunciation, and a
distinct manner in reading, as well as repeating.

Here, as every where, the main point to be attended to is, that every lesson, however short, may be perfectly learned, and the preceding portions repeated before entering on the next. Here, therefore, the master should not fail, as often happens, to employ competent teachers, and task them according to the capacity of the scholars, and carefully exact the task. The setting of tasks, as a trial of skill, and spur to diligence, should be often practised, the master having himself ascertained, by experiment, what the class can perform.

While the class are engaged in these exercises, they will have made considerable progress in the art of reading, and be qualified to proceed in the regular course of study; or, which is the same thing, as they go hand in hand, to enter—

§ 2. *On the course of moral and religious instruction.*

" Engage the mind in study, by a consideration of the Divine pleasures of truth and knowledge."—TEMPLE.

After having perused the first and second books, as directed in the foregoing Chapters, and thereby laid a foundation in the art of reading, the scholar proceeds to a regular course of study; or, as is the case in the National Schools, of moral and religious instruction. In this course, *Our Saviour's Sermon on the Mount* is entitled to indisputable pre-eminence. The inimitable System of Christian Morality, which it comprises, sets it above all price. The Evangelist describes the astonishment of the assembled multitude, on its delivery, in these words: " And it came to pass, when Jesus had ended these sayings, the people were astonished at his doctrine. For he taught them as one having authority, and not as the Scribes." Though it cannot be expected to make the same strong impression in a book, as from the lips of HIM, *who spake as never man spake,* yet, I am persuaded, it can never be read, as it ought to be read, without leaving an indelible conviction of the more than human wisdom of its Divine Author. This small tract the scholar studies as well as peruses; and does not proceed to another book, till he can read and explain it, distinctly and accurately. On the first perusal of this Discourse, he is examined in the meaning of every word,

I

member, and clause of every sentence, with the book open in his hands; and, on the second, with his book closed.

In the same manner are perused the following books, in succession;—*The Parables—Miracles—Discourses—and History of our blessed Saviour.* After these comes *Ostervald's* (admirable and concise) *Abridgement of the History of the Bible.* In this arrangement is seen an example of the simplification, method, and economy, which are leading features in the Madras School.

At the same time that the scholar is initiated in this course of study, extracted and abridged from the Old and New Testament, he learns by heart *the Catechism:* When he can *repeat* every question, in any order in which it can be put, in the most distinct, accurate, and perfect manner, he proceeds to a minute analysis and exposition of it. For this purpose, the *Catechism broken into short Questions,* will be found better adapted, perhaps, than all the explanations which have yet been given of it. It retains the original luminous diction, in which the most sublime precepts, and divine doctrines are conveyed. It alters nothing, but merely resolves every question into its simplest elements, after the manner of the daily examination of the Madras School, so as to present a single idea, at a time, to the mind—furnishing a model of that decomposition and division of labour, by which the most complex and difficult tasks may be rendered simple, and easy of acquisition. Then follow the *Chief Truths of the Christian Religion,* in question and answer, the larger expositions of the Catechism, &c.

It is a matter of frequent inquiry, how far instruction by books, composed in given questions and answers, should be carried. To this inquiry, a general reply may be made, that the rehearsal of answers from book, by rote, contributes little to the stock of knowledge, when, as often happens, it is no more than a memory of words, without understanding the sense. By reading history, for example, in this manner, the interest and chain of information are interrupted: words are pronounced, not things learnt. On the other hand, by examining the scholar, in the course of his studies, in every sentence, and much more if they examine one another by questions, put in every way, as they go along, you will certainly discover whether they understand what they read, and can instruct them wheresoever they are deficient. The questions are varied with the progress and attainments of the class, and frequently rise out of the answers which are made.

But it is objected, that the common run of masters of free-schools, and, of course, the teachers, are incapable of conducting such examinations. It is true that there may be such, just as there are masters, incapable of conducting a school to any advantage. But, whenever a master is equal to the one, he is not unequal to the other. It may be, indeed, that a master has had no practice in the method of examination, and, therefore, cannot perform it, when called upon, at random. The same is the case with the teacher and the scholar. By never analysing a sentence, or attending to its meaning, scarcely a sentence in a whole book is understood; whereas, by analysing one sentence, and doing it well, a great progress is made in understanding another. Commencing with what is simplest and easiest—the reading lessons of the 2d book of the National Society—the task of examination is rendered level to the meanest capacity. The illiterate master instructs himself as well as his scholars. By the daily analysis of the elementary lessons, their minds are gradually opened to the growing series of progressive study. The multiplication of questioning books is rendered unnecessary. Their end is far more effectually attained by the means here pointed out. The master, or teacher, or scholar, who does not learn, by this practice, to comprehend a sentence, will much less comprehend it by questioning books which actually lock up the mind, and preclude the growth of the understanding, by preventing its exercise. A happy and beautiful illustration of this subject is exhibited in the Central and other schools of the National Society, where the scholars examine one another, the teachers acting as umpires, and taking care that no fitting questions be omitted, and no unfit questions put.

The manner, in which the examination is conducted, may be exemplified in the first sentence of the *Sermon on the Mount.* In the first instance, the reading by pauses suggests a question at every intermission of the voice; thus, "*Jesus—seeing—the multitudes—went up—into a mountain.*" Whom did Jesus see? Who saw the multitudes? What did he then do? Who went up? Where did he go up? When did Jesus go up into a mountain? &c.

This minuteness of examination is discontinued as soon as the scholar is familiarized to it; and, as his comprehension enlarges, the questions are, by degrees, less numerous, and more general. After this manner, proceeding to the analysis of the Parables, each, in succession, helps to the comprehension of another; and a general notion of this popular and interesting form of conveying instruction, and also of the instruction conveyed, is attained. The teacher explains them in order to his class, as they were before explained to him, and examines them on every sentence, as he was himself before examined. He quits not one parable to go to another, till all of them are qualified to become instructors as far as they have gone, and actually do examine one another.

It seems unnecessary to dwell on the gradual effects of this progressive instruction, continued throughout the whole course of study. It is, therefore, earnestly recommended not to extend the use of books, composed in questions and answers, beyond a few elementary tracts, such as *The Catechism broken into short Questions; The Chief Truths of the Christian Religion, in question and answer*, which form a concise summary of Christianity. The specimens, exhibited in these models of the method of examination, will fully suffice to instruct every capable master in the art; and, if they do not, no questioning books will, in his hands, avail.

Thus, by means of the cheap and small tracts, which have been enumerated in this Chapter, the scholar is instructed not only to read, but also to understand what he reads. He is insensibly initiated in the first principles of Christianity, and attains an habitual acquaintance with them, which gives a readiness, distinctness, and pleasantness, to his future studies. Thus prepared, he enters on the study of the Bible, Prayer-book, &c., which he can now readily peruse at lengthened lessons, and derive instruction from the perusal, without previous spelling, or thumbing and wearing out the book. He first peruses the New Testament, and then the Old, and then again the New.

It is actually from not knowing how easy the communication and acquisition of knowledge may be rendered, by such a course of study, and such means, as are pointed out in this essay, and applied, as here applied, that the time spent in school is so often wasted to little or no purpose. In the way here pursued, the scholar has, in a few days, advanced one step, and acquired one species of knowledge, which renders the next step easier. Each preceding acquisition adds to the general stock, which more and more facilitates what follows; whereas, in slovenly and negligent teaching, the difficulties, never once surmounted, are still fresh, and meet him at every turn. In the Madras tuition, the difficulties diminish every day, as the scholar goes along from parable to parable, from parables to miracles, from miracle to miracle, from miracles to discourses, &c. By teaching one at a time, and well, the whole is soon learnt; by teaching the whole in a lump, nothing is well learnt.

The effect, though often exemplified, of reading these and other appropriate books at home, by the children, to their parents and relatives, &c. in keeping them out of the ale-house and gin-shop, and in impressing them with good principles and serious habits—it is not the business of these instructions in the art of teaching to expatiate upon.

But for what more particularly regards the intellectual, moral, and religious application of this System of Education, and the grand views which it opens to the Christian world—See the original Records of its rise, progress, and results. Elements of Tuition, vols. I. II. & III.

In conclusion, the parent, as well as the master, should keep in perpetual remembrance the *maxim*, which emphatically applies to early age and early culture—

" Neglectis urenda filix innascitur agris."
" In uncultivated lands noxious weeds spring up."

CHAP. VII. *On Arithmetic.*

"Arithmetic is of so general use in all the parts of life and business, that scarcely any thing is to be done without it."—LOCKE.

§ 1. *Preliminary Observations.*

Arithmetic has generally been considered as an intricate and difficult study, and not to be entered upon until the scholar has made considerable progress in reading and writing, and is somewhat advanced in years; and, as if to justify this erroneous notion, it is often taught in a manner, that places it beyond the reach of the infant mind, and even renders it unintelligible, as a science, to those of riper years.

The Madras System of Education, proceeding on juster principles, and a practical knowledge of the capacity and genius of children, treats them in every stage of the scholastic course, as rational creatures. In every lesson, it calls forth the exercise of their faculties, and the issue has demonstrated experimentally the truth of its positions. One of the first and most important is, that the acquisition of knowledge may be rendered easy and pleasant to the slenderest capacity, by a simple, methodical, and gradually progressive, course of study.

This position will be most readily and clearly elucidated in the study of a science, where every step admits of mathematical demonstration, and can be reduced to certainty. The child, therefore, enters on a course of arithmetic on the day of his admission into school, because it is a simple and beautiful science, and requires no previous knowledge of reading and writing. By carrying on its theory and practice together, it is happily adapted to the capacity of children, admirably calculated to open the infant faculties, to cultivate the growing understanding, and to gratify the love of method, of imitation, and of knowledge; at the same time it furnishes a manifest illustration of the principles, on which every branch of education is conducted in a Madras School. *There* no preliminary and artificial contrivances, which are, for the most part, more difficult of attainment than the branch of education itself, which they profess to facilitate and expedite, are admitted; and in conformity to the general rule, that prohibits all idle and unprofitable lessons, the learner begins at once with the object of his study.

Thus the science, here treated of, commences directly with the first elements of arithmetical progression, and with the practical exemplification of its rules, and proceeds, step by step, in a natural and uniform series of successive lessons*, such as the learner may not only readily comprehend, but, after a few examples, dictate for himself; and, while he is thus employed, he, in this act, learns to write the monades, (or digits, or single figures,) more effectually and sooner, by the interest which it gives to his lessons; nay, he can go through an elementary course of the four cardinal rules, which constitute the whole of arithmetic, with *understanding*, in less time than, in many schools, is allotted solely to write the idle digits, the mind being locked up all the while.

In the elements of arithmetic, as of reading and writing, two of the ablest, most active, expert, and trusty boys are selected, for the teacher of the lowest class, and for his assistant, who is also, in his absence, his substitute. As soon as may be, the class is paired off into tutors and pupils, the most forward boy being tutor to the most backward, &c.; and a superior tutor from a higher class is assigned to each scholar, (or to each pair, consisting of the pupil and his tutor of the class), an arrangement which is continued no longer, than till the children have acquired the use of their eyes and fingers, so far as to be able to copy, in legible characters, a few digits; after which the class can proceed of themselves, under their own teachers, without the superior tutors.

But the best way to surmount the difficulties of the initiatory lessons is, by uniting the class which have just learned them, to the class of beginners. The former, by revising their primary lessons, as tutors to the latter, while they greatly forward their pupils, by carrying them along with them, do at the same time most effectually advance their own improvement, by familiarising them-

---

* At home these lessons should be entered upon as soon as the child can be taught to form, ever so rudely, a digit, or a letter, in sand or on slate, which is at a much earlier age than is generally imagined.

selves with the first elements of their arithmetical studies; and each class, in turn, has the benefit of this arrangement.

§ 2. *Primary lessons, comprising an elementary course of Arithmetic.*

The tutors begin with teaching their pupils, at the desk, or on the form, to trace, and pronounce as they trace, over the prototype card (p. 89, supra) the prime digit, or cipher (0), and then to copy it on their slate*, and lastly, to enter it on the top of their slates, at the left-hand corner. This is the first lesson. From the *cipher*, (the *oriental root*) which has given its name to this science, springs the series of numbers, by the regular gradation of unity. Accordingly, every succeeding lesson consists in copying the former, and adding 1 to it, till they come to 9, or, in compliance with common practice, in forming arithmetical tables, to 12.†

Here each scholar of the class is instructed to mark the law of progression, as he goes along, and creates, as it were, for himself, the successive numbers. When the lesson is well known, and read at the desk, or on the bench, to the superior tutors, as directed in the reading lessons, the members of the class are then arranged on the floor, according to their performance, and rehearses it to the teacher and assistant. This done, they write and read the lesson, on the reverse or back of the slate, at their own dictation.

---

* At the commencement, particularly in families, for want of skill and experience on the part of the teacher, and of the new power and classification, and the motives and stimulants, of a Madras School, there is a difficulty in commanding that attention on the part of the child, which is requisite to form a figure or letter—a difficulty which frequently precludes him (or her) for years, from a natural and rational source of enjoyment and instruction; whereas, were this obstacle once removed by perseverance, and adequate motives and inducements presented to the infant mind, such as the parent alone can be a judge of, and by resolving, when necessary, a complex figure into minute parts, and teaching one at a time, every impediment to his progress would be soon surmounted. In case, however, of failing on slate, recourse may be had, in the outset, to the sand-board, by the proper use of which, the difficulty will be considerably lessened.

† The scholar may copy the numbers to 23, and then 34, 45, 56, 67, 78, 89, 100.

The following set of lessons will sufficiently explain the elementary course.

Primary lessons in forming the digits, and exhibiting the progression of numbers by unity.

1	2	3	4	5	6	7	8	9	10	11	12	13
0	0	0	0	0	0	0	0	0	0	0	0	0
1	1	1	1	1	1	1	1	1	1	1	1	1
	1	1	1	1	1	1	1	1	1	1	1	1
	1	1	1	1	1	1	1	1	1	1	1	1
		2	2	2	2	2	2	2	2	2	2	2
		1	1	1	1	1	1	1	1	1	1	1
			3	3	3	3	3	3	3	3	3	3
			1	1	1	1	1	1	1	1	1	1
				4	4	4	4	4	4	4	4	4
				1	1	1	1	1	1	1	1	1
					5	5	5	5	5	5	5	5
					1	1	1	1	1	1	1	1
						6	6	6	6	6	6	6
						1	1	1	1	1	1	1
							7	7	7	7	7	7
							1	1	1	1	1	1
								8	8	8	8	8
								1	1	1	1	1
									9	9	9	9
									1	1	1	1
										10	10	10
										1	1	1
											11	11
											1	1
												12

The numbers at top, 1, 2, 3, &c. denote the lessons or columns; the first lesson is 0; the second is 0 & 1 are 1; the third is 0 & 1 are 1, and 1 & 1 are 2, &c.; the child writing, & naming, and adding the figures, as he proceeds.

The class, having learned to write and read the digits, and to understand their value, proceed directly to a series of elementary lessons in addition and subtraction, multiplication and division, in all of which they actually instruct themselves, while, at the same time, and, in the same act, they compose and learn the addition and subtraction, multiplication and division tables. The diagrams will best explain and illustrate the processes.

Elémentary lessons in Addition and Subtraction, by which, at the same time, are formed and learned the Addition and Subtraction Tables.

Lesson 1

0	1	2	3	4	5	6	7	8	9	10	11	12
1	1	1	1	1	1	1	1	1	1	1	1	1
1	2	3	4	5	6	7	8	9	10	11	12	13
1	1	1	1	1	1	1	1	1	1	1	1	1
0	1	2	3	4	5	6	7	8	9	10	11	12

2

2	3	4	5	6	7	8	9	10	11	12
2	2	2	2	2	2	2	2	2	2	2
4	5	6	7	8	9	10	11	12	13	14
2	2	2	2	2	2	2	2	2	2	2
2	3	4	5	6	7	8	9	10	11	12

3

3	4	5	6	7	8	9	10	11	12
3	3	3	3	3	3	3	3	3	3
6	7	8	9	10	11	12	13	14	15
3	3	3	3	3	3	3	3	3	3
3	4	5	6	7	8	9	10	11	12

4

4	5	6	7	8	9	10	11	12
4	4	4	4	4	4	4	4	4
8	9	10	11	12	13	14	15	16
4	4	4	4	4	4	4	4	4
4	5	6	7	8	9	10	11	12

5

5	6	7	8	9	10	11	12
5	5	5	5	5	5	5	5
10	11	12	13	14	15	16	17
5	5	5	5	5	5	5	5
5	6	7	8	9	10	11	12

6

6	7	8	9	10	11	12
6	6	6	6	6	6	6
12	13	14	15	16	17	18
6	6	6	6	6	6	6
6	7	8	9	10	11	12

7

7	8	9	10	11	12
7	7	7	7	7	7
14	15	16	17	18	19
7	7	7	7	7	7
7	8	9	10	11	12

8

8	9	10	11	12
8	8	8	8	8
16	17	18	19	20
8	8	8	8	8
8	9	10	11	12

9

9	10	11	12
9	9	9	9
18	19	20	21
9	9	9	9
9	10	11	12

10

10	11	12
10	10	10
20	21	22
10	10	10
10	11	12

11

11	12
11	11
22	23
11	11
11	12

12

12
12
24
12
12

Elementary lessons in Multiplication and Division, by which, at the same time, are formed and learned the Multiplication and Division Tables.

Lesson 1
0	1	2	3	4	5	6	7	8	9	10	11	12
1	1	1	1	1	1	1	1	1	1	1	1	1
1)0	1	2	3	4	5	6	7	8	9	10	11	12
0	1	2	3	4	5	6	7	8	9	10	11	12

2
2	3	4	5	6	7	8	9	10	11	12
2	2	2	2	2	2	2	2	2	2	2
2)4	6	8	10	12	14	16	18	20	22	24
2	3	4	5	6	7	8	9	10	11	12

3
3	4	5	6	7	8	9	10	11	12
3	3	3	3	3	3	3	3	3	3
3)9	12	15	18	21	24	27	30	33	36
3	4	5	6	7	8	9	10	11	12

4
4	5	6	7	8	9	10	11	12
4	4	4	4	4	4	4	4	4
4)16	20	24	28	32	36	40	44	48
4	5	6	7	8	9	10	11	12

5
5	6	7	8	9	10	11	12
5	5	5	5	5	5	5	5
5)25	30	35	40	45	50	55	60
5	6	7	8	9	10	11	12

6
6	7	8	9	10	11	12
6	6	6	6	6	6	6
6)36	42	48	54	60	66	72
6	7	8	9	10	11	12

7
7	8	9	10	11	12
7	7	7	7	7	7
7)49	56	63	70	77	84
7	8	9	10	11	12

8
8	9	10	11	12
8	8	8	8	8
8)64	72	80	88	96
8	9	10	11	12

9
9	10	11	12
9	9	9	9
9)81	90	99	108
9	10	11	12

10
10	11	12
10	10	10
10)100	110	120
10	11	12

11
11	12
11	11
11)121	132
11	12

12
12
12
12)144
12

The class are examined by the teacher, or by one another, on each number of the tables as they proceed. They are carefully taught that if 2 and 3 are 5, then 3 and 2 must be 5; and 5 less 2 must be 3, and 5 less 3 must be 2: so that they may perceive the general principle, and render it unnecessary to ask, in future, any more than one out of these four questions, because any one of them being known, the other three are also known. Thus also in multiplication, which is a repeated addition, and division, which is a repeated subtraction, if 7 by 8 be 56, then 8 by 7 must be 56, and 7 in 56 must be 8, and 8 in 56 must be 7.

In examining, take from No. 5, examples: 5 and 6 are 11; 9 and 5 are 14; 12 less 5 is 7; and 10 less 5 is 5. And in multiplication, 5 by 7 is 35; 12 by 5 is 60; 5 in 50 is 10; and 5 in 25 is 5.

Every sum is proved; addition by subtraction; multiplication by division, and vice versâ. The proof exercises the class in the theory and practice of arithmetic, not less effectually than the primary operation. It habituates to accuracy. It is instructive and satisfactory by the result. Besides, by reversing the questions in addition and multiplication, it forms the easiest and most appropriate introduction to subtraction and division.

By observing the law of arithmetical progression in the dictation and formation of the tables, the memory is greatly assisted, and the child can repeat and learn, with understanding, his lessons, or tasks, at home, in his walks, and even whilst engaged in corporeal exercises, as well as at school. In the addition table, he marks the progression by unity. Ex. gr. In adding 4 to 4, 5, 6, &c. the sums are respectively 8, 9, 10, &c.; and in multiplying, the products increase by the number of units in the multiplicand—thus, 4, 5, 6, multiplied by 4, the products are respectively 16, 20, 24. The thorough and ready acquaintance with the elementary lessons, that constitute the addition and multiplication tables, (which are thus easily and satisfactorily attained, whilst the child has been engaged in performing the elementary lessons) greatly facilitates and expedites every subsequent operation.

§ 3. *On Numeration and Notation.*

All the while the child has been learning Notation and Numeration by writing and reading numbers as far as 144. He may now be practised in writing and reading all the varieties which occur in a half period, or number consisting of three places, viz. units, tens, and hundreds, according to the use and place of the cipher. Of units there is only one case, as 7; of tens, two, as 70, 77; of hundreds, four, as 700, 707, 770, 777; or, varying the figures, 7, 40, 96, 700, 408, 390, 521; these seven cases, viz. 6; 20, 38; 200, 608, 540, 937, include all the varieties which can occur in writing any number, not exceeding three figures, or half a period. Now, every number, however long, is composed of a repetition of half periods. In these elements, therefore, viz. in reading and writing units, tens, and hundreds, or a single half period, the scholar is made perfect. No more is necessary to enable him to read and write the longest number, which is only a succession of half periods.

The difficulty and waste of time, in counting units, tens, hundreds, thousands, tens of thousands, hundreds of thousands, millions, &c.; and in beginning to write down long numbers from the right, to the left, are superseded by a simple contrivance, which renders numeration and notation plain and easy. This consists in dividing every long number into half periods, of three places each, and periods, of six places each, by alternate commas and semicolons, and putting respectively 1, 2, 3, 4, &c. dots, or these numbers themselves, over the right-hand figures of the periods, beginning with the second period from the right. Instead of proceeding, as usual, to a multiplicity of examples, gradually increasing in length, a single one (the longer the easier) will include all the shorter, and teach numeration at one step. Thus to read:

7 3 8 0 7 9 0 0 0 4 8 0 0 5 6 7 0 0 0 0 5 9 8 4 2 0 0 7 0 8 0 1

mark as follows:

73; 807,900; 048,005; 670,000; 598,420; 070,801:

And read, first the divisions, one by one, each by itself, as if it was a single half period, thus, seventy-three; eight hundred and seven; nine hundred; forty-eight; five; six hundred and seventy; five hundred and ninety-eight; four hundred and twenty; seventy; eight hundred and one: and then, precisely in the same manner, only pronouncing thousands for each comma, and lastly, with the addition of millions, for, every dot; thus—Seventy-three millions of M. of M. of M. of M. (or quintillions); eight hundred and seven thousand, nine hundred M. of M. of M. of M. (or quartillions); forty-eight thousand, and five M. of M. of M. (or trillions); six hundred and seventy thousand M. of M. (or billions); five hundred and ninety-eight thousand, four hundred and twenty millions; seventy thousand; eight hundred, and one.

Numeration thus taught, notation may be said to be already learnt. The distinguishing marks enable the scholar to begin to write down the number, at the left hand, without previously counting, units, tens, &c. An example will suffice. Note down, seventy septillions, eighty thousand quadrillions, five hundred billions, and four thousand and ten,

7   6   5   4   3   2
70 ; 000,000 ; 000,000 ; 080,000 ; 000,000 ; 000,500 ;
    1
000,000 ; 004,010.

§ 4. *General Directions and Suggestions.*

The class, having thus gone through a concise and comprehensive series of lessons, returns to addition, and commences a methodical and practical course of arithmetic. The lessons are performed on the floor; and, when the scholar writes with pen and ink, entered, at the desk, in a book. The teacher dictates, extempore, a sum, and the whole class set it down upon their slates, having no other copy than the script prototype card. They then read the sum given out, in order to correct it if necessary; after which they perform the operation, each taking a single step by turn. When the whole is performed and proved, the teacher inspects the slates, assigns his due rank to each member of the class, and sets the scholar, who has not written the sum, or any part of it, correctly and properly, to copy it, with the assistance of a tutor, from a slate, on which it is correct, till it is well done.

After two or three initiatory lessons, the sums are dictated by the scholars themselves, each in succession giving out a minute portion *. Several classes, consisting of hundreds of boys, may be employed in the same arithmetical operation on the floor, at one and the same time, a single voice only being uttered in succession, as called upon by the teacher, and all the rest setting down the figure from the mouth of the successive speaker—each teacher taking charge of his respective class.

For the sake of acquiring the habit of readiness and quickness, it is useful for each child, when a sum has been given out, to perform it individually in his place, and take his rank according to his despatch in the performance.

The larger the classes the better. A class considerably inferior, being joined in the ranks of a superior, and repeating with them, and copying from the slates of the boys, next to whom they are placed, will soon be able to keep pace with them.

The advantage of the processes which have been described is, not only that the most numerous class are instructed with a facility, far greater than a single scholar can be taught in the usual mode of proceeding; but that no scholar can be one moment inattentive or idle; and every one must necessarily be master of every rule in which he has been instructed, or rather, has instructed himself: nor can he (as so often happens in the old school) forget the operations, to which the principle, whereby he performed them of his own accord, is a perpetual remembrancer, or guide.

In the National Schools, the application of the compound rules is chiefly confined to pounds, shillings, pence,

---

* When they give out the lessons for themselves, they seldom attend to variety, or dictate the cipher or higher digits, but chiefly the lower, 1, 2, 3, 4, except especially instructed—an error which often passes for years unnoticed by the teachers, master, and visitors.

and farthings*; the tables commonly used for this purpose may be dispensed with. It is only necessary to
instruct the child, how many of one denomination make
one of another: that 4 farthings make a penny, 12 pence
a shilling, and 20 shillings a pound, and so of other tables.
The division table does the rest. Thus, 27 pence divided
by 12, is 2*s.* 3*d.* &c.

It is thought unnecessary to spend time in learning
tables of weights and measures, which are in general soon
forgotten. A few examples in cases of the most common occurrence may suffice, from which the use of the
rest will be sufficiently obvious, when occasion calls for
them.

On the whole, for the application of the preceding hints,
I must refer to a Madras School, for an illustration of its
peculiar processes. I only observe once more, that the
method of Madras Instruction in classes is happily and
beneficially exemplified in teaching every process in arithmetic; and that if the master and scholar are made
familiar with the elementary principle and practices,
they themselves can *then* apply them to the different
rules, which are found in any plain book of arithmetic.
All that they have to do, is to substitute the *new* for the
old methods.

I must not, however, conclude this chapter, without
remarking, that the great desideratum is, to have a
System of Arithmetic composed on Madras principles,
for the higher orders of schools, and printed in script,
which may serve for their copies in writing, as well as
for their instruction in arithmetic.

---

* In adding the column of shillings, the scholar proceeds, as in
simple addition, setting down the right-hand figure in the sum of the
units in its proper place, and carrying the left-hand figures to the tens,
the sum of which being divided by 2, the remainder, if any, is set
down in the place of tens, and the quotient carried to the pounds. In
like manner in land measure, in carrying at 40, divide by 4; and so in
every case of an even number of tens.

In proving addition, when the top line is cut off, the scholar, in
adding the others, begins at the uppermost of them, to vary the
process.

It would be to go beyond the design of this elementary treatise,
to notice specific operations, or contractions; *e. g.* multiplying or

CHAP. VIII.—*On Economy.*

§ 1. " It is worth observing, that every improvement of our System has been attended with a diminution of expense." p. 123

For particulars relative to the economy of the first experiment of this System, both as to money and time, see p. 42, supra, and p. 34—7, 46—9, and 51—2, of the Madras Report.

1. The great economy of this System may be illustrated by an imaginary case. Suppose, that in two empires, consisting each of 2,000,000 children, to be educated; the one on the old plan, in schools of 50 pupils each, the other on the new, of 500, at the stipend of £50 to each master. The amount of school fees, in the one case, would be £1 a scholar; or £2,000,000 — in the other, 2s. a scholar, or £200,000—the difference being £1,800,000. But, allowing the Madras master double this stipend, the difference would then be £1,600,000. What may not yet be done, when men's minds are opened to the requisite measures for this purpose? Though this ideal case does not admit of being realized to the extent of the hypothesis, an application of this principle, according to circumstances, would be attended with corresponding benefits.

2. Again, suppose that the school meets 6 hours a day, and that the master, on the one plan, teaches a considerable portion of his scholars individually, and the rest in small classes, making together 20 *separate divisions*, to be instructed by himself alone. In this case, on an average, he could only give 18 *minutes* a day to each child. The Madras master, on the contrary, by himself and his teachers, may be said to give 360 *minutes* to each child, or in proportion of 20 to 1. What use, on this ground alone, making every allowance can be desired, might not be made of such an advantage!

3. Other branches of economy are, the frequent use of slates and pencils for pen, ink, and paper, and of small

---

dividing by 10, 100, 1000 &c. which is only to annex 1, 2, 3, &c. ciphers to the multiplicand, and to cut off as many places in the dividend, &c.

and cheap tracts, comprising no more than, and all that, is necessary for the purpose; and *perfect instruction*, by which one page goes as far as half a dozen read in a careless and slovenly manner.

§ 2. The following is a list of small tracts, made up in sets of 50 each, which may be had at the reduced prices here stated, by application, in writing, from any subscriber of the Society for Promoting Christian Knowledge, addressed to the Secretary, Bartlett's-buildings. The shop prices are also set down.

	Selling Prices.			Reduced Prices.		
50 dozen leaves Central School Book*, No. 1	0	8	4	0	4	2
50 National Society Central School Book, No. 2	0	8	0	0	2	0
50 Sermon on the Mount	0	8	0	0	2	0
50 Parables of our blessed Saviour	0	8	0	0	2	0
50 Miracles	0	8	0	0	2	0
50 Discourses	0	8	0	0	2	0
50 History	0	8	0	0	2	0
50 Ostervald's Abridgt of the Bible	0	8	0	0	2	0
50 Broken Catechism	0	10	0	0	3	1
50 Chief Truths of the Christian Religion	0	8	0	0	2	0
Total for 50 children				£1	3	3

Which amounts to less than 6*d.* for each child.

But as, under good management, each of these small tracts will, on an average, serve six children, in succession, the real expense of books for suitable instruction in the art of reading, and in the first rudiments of religion, cannot be estimated at more than 1*d.* for each child.

The Author begs leave to recommend to private families and schools, where the funds admit of it, to read, in the first instance, and preparatory to the study of the Bible,

	Selling Prices.		Reduced Prices.	
Mrs. Trimmer's Abridgment of the New Testament	1	8	0	11
Ditto of the Old	2	0	1	3

Her other books for private families will be found highly useful.

---

* See Script Cards, substituted for this book, pp. 82, 92.

§ 3. *Slates and Pencils.* Unframed slates, polished on both sides, are Sold by G. ROAKE, 31, Strand.

Slates, 7 inches by 5		at	2	6 per dozen.
———— 6½	4¼	at	2	8
———— 6	4	at	1	9
Dutch slate pencils		6	0 per 1000	
Black lead ditto		1	0 per dozen	

§ 4. Lastly: *In building and fitting-up school-rooms,* the following hints are said to " *combine the greatest convenience with the least expense.*"

For school-rooms, the common allowance is seven (not less than six) square feet for each child; but the larger the better, as far as ten feet. A barn is accounted a model of a school-room. It only wants windows, the bottom of which should be about five feet from the floor, and should open at the top; or else there should be apertures at the top of the walls (or ceiling) for ventilation. To prevent echo—a frequent nuisance in new schools, the roof may be without ceiling—walls lime-washed— no stucco, plastering, domes, or circular walls.

The expense of building varies so much in different places, that no general estimate can be made. The fitting-up costs but little. All that is necessary is a few plain forms, and a ledge or desk, for writing on, against the wall, along all the sides of the room.

By this simple and convenient disposition of the cheap furniture of a school-room, there is accommodation for one-half more children than by the usual method of placing the tables, desks, and forms, in the body of the room.

CHAP. IX.—*On Registers and Weekly Examinations.*

§ 1. There are no less than six forms of registers prepared for some schools :—

1. *The Admission Book* contains each child's number, name, age, dates of entering and leaving school, parents' names, occupation, residence, and a column for remarks.

2. *The Marked Book* is kept by the teacher and assistant of each class, whose names are written, with ink, on the front page; also the rank of the class, and the date when the book is taken in hand. The teacher also dates with pencil, where the lesson begins, every morning, and marks the end of each lesson when given out, thus ⌈.

In writing individually, each child dates his copy and ciphering book, in small figures, where the daily lessons begin.

3. *An Alphabetical List* of the scholars' names is necessary in large schools, for a reference to the admission book.

4. *The Daily Attendance Book* shews the number of boys present, absent with or without leave, and the total number. A slate with these entries is, an hour after meeting, morning and evening, hung up in a conspicuous part of the room, for the inspection of the visitors.

5. *The Class Book* contains, at one end, the place each scholar holds at the close of the school, and at the other, the employment of the class. In the fluctuation of scholars in the classes of a large school, this register is of little use as a general reference beyond a few weeks. It may suffice for each teacher to keep it for his exercise and immediate guidance.

6. *The Paidometer* shews each child's monthly progress, from his admission into the school, to leaving it, in twelve triple columns, in which, on the last day of every month, are entered the book, page, and stage of the course at which the scholar is arrived in his reading, ciphering, and religious rehearsals. A single line on a folio sheet, comprehends the progress of each child for a year.

These simple contrivances are fitted to correct idleness, and detect negligence in their origin, and to bear permanent testimony of merit and demerit, even if overlooked in passing.

Of these registers, *the marked book* is indispensably requisite as a guide, a check, and an instrument of discipline. Without it, the master cannot, while he is present with one class, ascertain with any precision, what, in the mean-time, has been done in the others. So essential is it to the performance of his functions with fidelity, that the neglect or inaccuracy of it generally indicates the first symptoms of inattention to the school, and should instantly be corrected by the visitor. If not, the school may be expected to fall off daily.

The *paidometer* will form a record of facts of no less value in the intellectual, than the barometer, thermometer, &c. in the physical world. It deserves the particular attention of all those, who take an interest in the success of their own schools, and in the cause of general education.

Its importance needs no illustration; it furnishes immediate and indelible information, relative to the progress of every child, throughout his literary career, and is eminently fitted to stimulate exertion on the part of the master, and to enable the visitors to check, correct, and regulate, the progress of the scholars. The scholastic world will be put in possession of a mass of materials, the basis of a new science, and, in course of time, a criterion will be obtained, by which visitors may judge of the comparative progress of their school, with that of other schools; and an average standard established, by which the master may ascertain his own success, by the success of others, and be stimulated to exertion. But the strictest provision must be made, that no book be passed without perfect instruction. The visitors, therefore, should ascertain, by actual examination, whether the report be faithfully made, the entry literally correct, and the scholar intimately acquainted with all that goes before the stages, at which he is stated to have arrived.

This register may be rendered eminently useful, and has a peculiar claim to the attention of visitors. It will, as has been said, hold up to the inspectors, as well as master, a mirror of his diligence and exertion.—form a standard of reference, for the use of schools and families —and supply a collection of facts, for the history of the development of the human faculties, of infinite value to the philosophy of mind.

§ 2. *An examination* of the school should take place once a week, at which it is of great importance that the visitors and superintendent be present. The examination commences with the inspection of the copy and ciphering books and slates, arranged as specified (see p. 84, supra); after which, the slates are taken up and wiped, and the classes are, in turn, examined on any part of the lessons of the week. No interruption is given to the daily business, which, though the school is said to be stopt, goes on in silence, all the classes, not under examination, writing at their desks, or on the floor. But for this contrivance, the instruction of the Central School would be subject to perpetual interruption from the incessant flow of company, and examination of particular classes, for which the omnipotent machinery of the New School could alone have provided the remedy.

The easiest and surest method of ascertaining the state of a school, by visitors unacquainted with the System, is simply calling (what is rarely done) the roll of the latest admissions, from the admission-book, or inspecting the paidometer, and marking the progress they have made, and examining them in the book at which the scholars have arrived.

The increase and diminution of numbers, is an almost infallible criterion of the state of the school; which may be also known by the master imputing every fault to the badness of his teachers and scholars, and by his not being conscious that they always are what he makes them. p. 72, supra.

By the proportion of scholars who cannot write and read the first book, as well as by the performance of those who are further advanced, the master, visitors, and all concerned, may judge of the character and progress of their school; and in case of any failure or imperfection, take steps for correction.

CHAP. X. — *On Schools for the richer Classes of the Community, and higher Branches of Study.*

Not only the universal principle and general laws of the New School, but most, if not all, of what has gone before, apply, with very little alteration, to tuition, in every branch of education, in every art and science, and is no less adapted to knitting, needle-work, the workshop, the prison*, the police, agriculture, and the operations of a manufactory, than to the economy of a school.

---

* Thus to take an example from a prison. With ingenuous and innocent children in a School, it is a system of prevention, of fostering, and of progressive improvement: but, with criminals in a prison, it is a system of restraint, correction, and reformation.

§ 1. *On Grammar and Classical Schools.*

"I would recommend it to teachers to take particular care, that, after the manner of nurses, they nourish the tender mind, and allow it to be filled with the milk, as it were, of agreeable instruction." QUIN.

"Give me a boy who is roused by praise; whom glory delights, and who cries when vanquished. This boy will be fostered by ambition, he will be stung by reproach, and animated by a sense of honour. In him I will entertain no apprehension of sloth."— QUIN.

Such is 'the language of the great master of antiquity; and all the moderns, as well as ancients, agree with him. But the New System has, in this as in other respects, led to a deeper insight into the infant faculties, and has given birth to new facts. It can now be truly said—

"Give me (almost) any boy, and let me plant him in a Madras School, properly regulated and conducted, and I will, in a great degree, shew you these fruits. None shall remain insensible to the impulses which are there given, and to the motives which are there presented to the mind. In none shall remain dormant the principles of humanity, implanted in all. In all shall the love of imitation, and a sense of honour and shame, develop themselves, and display their powerful influence."— *Ludus Literarius*, p. 185.

"When Crates saw an ignorant boy, he struck his tutor."

In the Report of the Madras Asylum (1796), the Author recommended, that the experiment, which had been attended with such signal success in that school, should be tried " *in every charity or free school,—and in the generality of public schools and academies.*" Report, p. 53 and p. 43 supra.

After further experience, he expressed himself in stronger terms.

"He will be a sturdy master of an academy, who shall make the first trial; but could he once overcome prejudice and opposition, which I do not advise him to attempt, unless he feel his own powers equal to the Augean task, and achieve the arrangement according to this scheme, with his scholars themselves; and, were he endued with due perseverance, I could venture to promise him success beyond any expectation they can entertain, who have never witnessed the wonderful effects of this System. I can ensure to him, under its just and impartial administration, the hearts of his scholars, and, by consequence, the heads of their parents."—*Analysis*, 1807.

"Of classical and other schools for the higher orders, on this system, the number is not known, and is supposed to be but few*. These few, however, furnish respectable specimens of the " *Ludus Literarius.*" For three of them, Latin Grammars are composed, and published by the masters.

"The first and foremost is one of our great schools. Of this school the Author cannot express any part of what he thinks, and what he feels. About seven [now eleven] years ago, on the first mention by the head master, of his wish to introduce the Madras System into his school, the Author warned him of many difficulties, discouragements, and dangers, which he must expect to encounter, and of the probable loss of scholars at the outset; but added, that, if he persevered, he would ensure him two for every one he lost. The event has surpassed all expectation. The number of scholars is nearly trebled, and would have been far greater, if there had been due accommodation.

" The Author remained in town, for some time after the day fixed for his departure, in order to see a proof sheet of the first Latin Grammar, composed entirely on the principle of the *Ludus Literarius* (consisting of accidence, vocabulary, and syntax), and to introduce the Madras System into one department of the school, by giving to a head class a lesson in arithmetic on this plan.

" On his return to town, after the *Ludus Literarius* had been in action for six months, he was informed, that not a single corporal punishment had been inflicted during that period, on the score of learning (a rare event!) and that no scholar had passed over a single lesson without being master of it (a still rarer event!)

" The Author does not presume to offer any opinion of his own on the character of this school, or on the ability, enthusiasm, resolution, perseverance, and discretion, with which the *Ludus Literarius* is carried on. He has observed, at the annual examinations which he has attended, with infinite delight, the astonishment and admiration of the visitors.

" The chaste and correct reports, with which the OFFICIAL EXAMINERS have favoured the Author, will give some idea of the effects produced in this school by the Madras System. By giving publicity to them, he conceives, that he shall best promote the common object."—*Vindication of Children,* 1819, p. 83—5.

This School has gone on progressively to this day, the number being now nearly 500—all for whom there is accommodation: and the excellent Grammar has gone through several editions.

For the letters of Dr. Mant (Bishop of Killaloe) and

---

* Their numbers have increased and are gradually increasing.

Dr. D'Oyley, then Chaplains to the Archbishop of Canterbury, on this most important subject, see p. 85—7, Ib.

For other Grammar and English Schools, see p. 87 —95, Ib.; and *Instructions, &c. for conducting Schools,* sixth edition, 1817, p. 34-5, 135—7.

Since these publications, a recent case has occurred, entitled to particular notice. In little more than one year, an old Grammar School, having been converted into a Madras School, has grown from 14 to 100—the com- -plement to which the Preceptor (Rev. Dr. Bond, Hanwell) had restricted himself. Nor can there be a doubt with similar measures, by future adventurers, corresponding success will ensue.

But it is only further necessary, under this head, to refer to *Elements of Tuition, Part III., Ludus Litera- rius—the Classical and Grammar School*—a volume entirely devoted to the interesting question on the application of the Madras System to the higher order of children, in whose breasts the sentiments of a virtuous and generous emulation are predominant. There the principles of the New System are demonstrated and defended—objections answered—the plan of a Latin (and consequently Greek) Grammar laid down, *Lilye's and Eton Grammars* analysed, and the necessary details for conducting education, set forth at full length.

§ 2. *Ladies' Boarding Schools.*

In these schools, the Madras System shines with peculiar lustre. Early and beautiful specimens are seen at Miss Walker's School, Leamington; Miss Tabrum's (now Mrs. Tabrum's) School, Clapton House; and the Clergy Orphan School, under Miss Woods, St. John's Wood, Regent's Park; for all of which, see *Instructions,* &c. 1817, p. 60—1, and p. 135—7.

§ 3. *Schools of Industry.*

In Girls' Schools of Industry on the Madras Plan, every thing is conducted as in the school of letters. The knitting and needle-work, and whatever else is taught, are arranged from easy to difficult. Each class has its teacher, who often works herself, while she attends and examines her pupils, or while they read, by turns, to one another. Every day the scholars have places assigned

L

to them, according to the relative quantity and quality of the work done, of which the amount is registered. Boys' schools of industry are conducted on the same principle. All the schools for the poor, should be schools of industry. See *Analysis*, 1805, p. 79; and *Elements of Tuition, Part II.—the English School*, p. 411—422; and for a Sketch of a National Institution for training up the Children of the Poor: and Mr. Pitt and Mr. Whitbread's Bills for Schools of Industry. Ib. pp. 422—433.

———

" In bidding farewell to this publication, I am unable, either to pass over in silence, or to express, as I ought, the debt of gratitude, due for the support and furtherance which the Madras System of Education has long derived from the zealous patronage, extensive bounty, and personal labours, of a Noble Friend, deeply versed in its spirit, its principles, and its practices. My Lord Kenyon is continually occupied in its diffusion and advancement, as the most effectual means of GOOD TO MAN, and GLORY TO GOD on earth." *Instructions.* &c. 1817, p. 137.

———

POSTSCRIPT.

§ 1. *Original Pupils of Madras Asylum.*

The substance of the documents, referred to in the Note, p. 3, of the Introduction, and the argument there founded on them, are thus summed up by the Rev. F. Iremonger, in his " SUGGESTIONS TO THE PROMOTERS OF DR. BELL'S SYSTEM OF EDUCATION, LONGMAN, 1813,"—a work, abounding with useful and solid information. " The Author (says he) cannot conclude this introductory chapter, without congratulating the original inventor of the System, Dr. Bell, on the realization of his anxious hopes, on the reward of those labours, which will, under divine Providence, prove a lasting blessing to posterity, and call forth the gratitude of thousands in this Country, stimulated by the same feelings of affection, which, after eleven years' silence, produced from his Indian pupils a letter, fully proving, (as Dr. Bell says) ' that the sentiments, which it was his incessant aim to inspire, had not evaporated; and that the principles, which his dutiful pupils had imbibed, had taken deep root, and continued to yield their natural fruits.'

" This pleasing instance of gratitude, as well as satisfactory practical proof of the strong hold, which the new System takes on the mind, is signed by nearly fifty of his pupils at Madras, (in the name of the whole body) and, while it shews a becoming gratitude, on their part, for the unwearied assiduity shewn by their benevolent pastor, it enumerates the respectable situations in life, in which they are placed, ascribing to his paternal care, under the great Disposer of events, their preservation, their comfort, and all the valuable advantages they enjoyed. They have since presented Dr. Bell with a service of sacramental plate, and a gold chain, and a medal, and have begged that 100 copies of his miniature, on copper-plate engravings, may be sent to be distributed amongst them. When the total ignorance of those children, at the time of their first being instructed by Dr. Bell, is considered, the lamentable want of early good impressions, and their exposure to vice, and particularly deceit of every kind; and when we compare their subsequent moral and religious improvement, and the respectable places in society, which they afterwards filled; when too there was more to undo, before sound principles could be imbibed, than can be the case in this happier Country, an undeniable proof is afforded of the excellence of Dr. Bell's mode of instruction; nor can there be the smallest reason for doubting, that, whenever the same measures are steadily and perfectly adopted, they will be attended uniformly with the same lasting good effects."

The former of these documents, having been communicated to the Court of Directors of the East India Company, at the request of one of their body, were by them acknowledged as follows :—

" Sir,—I have received and laid before the Court of Directors of the East India Company, your letter to Mr. Ramsay of the 5th instant, with the documents from your India pupils, accompanying the same, and I am commanded to express to you the high satisfaction the perusal of those documents have afforded the Court, in learning therefrom, how much the valuable Institution, over which you lately presided at Madras, has benefitted by your labours and talents.

" I am further commanded to convey to you the Court's thanks for the perusal of the documents in question, which are herewith returned. I have the honour to be, Sir, your most obedient humble Servant,

" JAMES COBB, Assistant Secretary.

" _East India House_, 13th October, 1812.
" The Rev. Dr. Bell."

§ 2. _Original School Committee of National Society._

In Chap. VIII., on the Sketch of History, the following document was omitted.

" At a meeting of the general Committee of the National Society, held at St. Martin's Library, 22d January, ~~1801~~. *1812*

" Resolved, that Dr. Bell be requested to act, under the direction of this Society, as superintendent in the formation and conduct of the Central, and other Schools, to be established by this Society, in the Metropolis, and its vicinity, with power to engage such persons, as masters and mistresses, as shall be adequate to carry the purposes of this Society into effect; and to retain, suspend, or dismiss such masters and mistresses.

" 2dly—That Dr. Bell be empowered to engage persons to be trained as masters and mistresses.

" 3dly—That the Trustees of the several schools of Lambeth, Mary-le-bone, and Gower's Walk, Whitechapel, be immediately applied to by the School Committee, to be hereafter appointed, to enable this Society to give Dr. Bell sufficient power to train masters in those schools, according to the former resolution to this effect.

" 4thly—That a Sub-Committee be appointed for the general management of the Central, and other schools, and to assist Dr. Bell in carrying into execution the foregoing Resolutions; and that such Committee do consist of the Lord Bishop of Salisbury, the Right Honourable Lord Radstock, the Right Honourable Sir John Nicholl, the Rev. Dr. Barton, and William Davis, Esq., three of whom to be a quorum.

" 5thly—That Dr. Bell do report his proceedings, from time to time, to such Committee; and that such report be submitted to this Committee."

---

§ 3. *Bishop Porteus's Pastoral Letter, and Negro Slaves.*

Note to p. 34, after " benighted and barbarous nations."

Having also omitted to record, in its proper place, any particulars of the (almost) numberless schools established in foreign parts, it remains to refer for details on this head to the Reports of the National Society,—of the British and Foreign School Society, and—of the Society of Elementary Education, Paris, &c.

It is, also, deemed advisable to produce here an early and late example, on interesting occasions, as specimens. It is due to the memory of the late Dr. Porteus, to introduce, for the first specimen, extracts from the *Postscript* and *Appendix* of a Pastoral

" Letter (recommending the education of the negro-slave children) to the Governors, Legislators, and Proprietors of Plantations in the British West India Islands," by the Right Rev.

Bailby Porteus, D. D. Bishop of London. Cadell and Davis
London, 1808.

P. 35. " Dr. Bell, (the original Author of such Schools on
the New System) is, as you will see in the Appendix, decidedly
of opinion, that *Sunday Schools*, well conducted, will fully answer
the purpose of instructing the negro children, both in reading
and in religion.... The expense, as Dr. Bell states it, will be
reduced to a mere nothing, a sum below all notice."

P. 37. " *Appendix; containing a Short Sketch of the New
System of Education for the Poor, in a Letter from the Rev. Dr.
Bell, (the Inventor of that System,) to the Lord Bishop of London.*"
—" The measure planned by your Lordship, was alone wanted
to crown the long and successful struggle (the abolition of the
slave-trade) which you have made in the cause of suffering humanity; and the time will come, when this measure, formed for
the completion of your great design, will also succeed. * * * *
If the humble System of Education, which was founded and
reared in the Eastern World, and thence imported into Europe,
be now, by your Lordship's exertions, happily transferred to the
Western World; and should it, in the one Indies, prove as
instrumental in promoting the benevolent purposes which your
Lordship has so much at heart, as it has been in the other, in
promoting the views of the Honourable the East-India Directors,
and the Government of Madras, I shall think I have not lived
in vain."

In sending a youthful parishioner of the Author's, to
introduce the Madras System of Education into schools
for the negro slaves in the West Indies, his Lordship
wrote to the Author as follows :—

" *It is a big word to say,* but he will do as much good in the
Western world, as Buonaparte is doing mischief in the European
world."

At that time his Lordship often said that, till this work
was accomplished, he considered his victory in the long
and arduous struggle for the abolition of the slave-trade,
as incomplete.

§ 4. *Native School of African Negro.*
The following is the late specimen alluded to :
In a letter to the Rev. W. Johnson, dated Annamaboo,
10th July, 1822, John Anderson, an African Negro,
trained at Baldwin's Gardens, gives an account of his
teaching, with good success, a Native School, to which
he was appointed by Sir Charles Mac Carthy, Governor
of Sierra Leone.

§ 5. *Conclusion of Instructions for conducting Regimental Schools.*

Note to p. 32 and 51. The conclusion of the ' IN-
STRUCTIONS FOR ESTABLISHING AND CONDUCTING
REGIMENTAL SCHOOLS,' will not be considered as mis-
placed here.

' The attention of every person, directing and superintending
a school, is particularly called to watch over the moral and religious conduct of the children; and to implant in them, as well
by daily practice, as by perfect instruction in the books recommended for that purpose, such habits as may best conduce to
guard them against the vices to which their condition is peculiarly liable. In particular, the most rigid observance should
be enforced of the grand virtue of truth, both for it own sake,
and as supplying one of the readiest means of correcting vice of
every kind. On this ground, a lie should never be excused; and
a fault, aggravated by a lie, should always be punished with
exemplary severity.

' Those portions of their religious books should be strongly
rivetted in their minds, which warn against lying, swearing, theft,
idleness, provoking conduct, and the use of improper expressions,
one towards another; and which are fitted to impress on them,
from their earliest years, the principles of our holy religion, as
established in this kingdom, being the surest means of promoting
their success in their various pursuits in this world, and of ensuring
their EVERLASTING HAPPINESS.'

§ 6. *Valedictory Request.* Finally, I beg leave, once
more, to implore the attention of trustees and managers
of schools to a FIRST PRINCIPLE, that, in the *management of a school,* (as in all the affairs of life,) it is *expedient
to unite the duty and interest of the master: In one shape
or other, then, let the master's stipend or emoluments be
dependent on the proficiency, happiness, and number of
his pupils,*—not, indeed, on the absolute number, for it
is as easy for a master of ability to teach 500 as 50, but
on the increase or diminution of numbers, consequent on
the good or ill conduct of the school.

THE END.

R. CLAY, Printer, 9, Devonshire-street, Bishopsgate.

Works by the Author,

SOLD BY G. ROAKE, 31, STRAND.

1. ELEMENTS of TUITION, Part (Vol.) 1,—THE MÀDRAS SCHOOL; or the Report of the Military Male Orphan Asylum at Madras, with its original Proofs and Vouchers: as transmitted from India in 1796, and published in London 1797, under the title of "*An Experiment in Education made at the Male Asylum of Madras —Suggesting a System by which a School or Family may teach itself under the Superintendence of the Master or Parent.*" A literal Reprint: to which are subjoined additional Documents and Records, illustrative of the progress of the new System of education in the School in which it originated, and of its fruits in the character, conduct, and fortunes of its pupils. 4s. Dedicated, by permission, to Field Marshal His Royal Highness the DUKE of YORK.

II. ELEMENTS of TUITION, Part (Vol.) 2,—THE ENGLISH SCHOOL; or the History, Analysis, and Application of the Madras System of Education to English Schools. A new Edition, greatly enlarged. 12s. Dedicated, by permission, to His Royal Highness the PRINCE REGENT. 1814.

III. ELEMENTS of TUITION, Part (Vol.) 3,—LUDUS LITERARIUS; the Classical and Grammar School; or an Exposition of an Experiment in Education, made at Madras in the years 1789-1796: with a view to its introduction into Schools for the Higher Orders of Children, and with particular suggestions for its application to a *Grammar School.* 12s. Dedicated to the Honourable and Right Reverend SHUTE, Lord BISHOP of DURHAM. 1815.

A SERMON on the EDUCATION of the POOR, under an appropriate System, preached at Lambeth, 28th June, 1807. 2d Edition. 1s. Dedicated, by permission, to His Grace the ARCHBISHOP of CANTERBURY.

A VINDICATION of CHILDREN, addressed to Parents, Tutors, &c. and also to Legislators and Governors. With an Appendix, containing the Author's Scholastic Tour on the Continent, &c. 8vo. 3s.

In these volumes, the Madras System of Education is traced from its origin: and its unexampled effects in promoting the happiness and improvement of its Pupils, and its fitness, in the words of the National Society, to give "a new character to society at large," are illustrated in theory, and exemplified in practice.

A LIST

OF

STATIONERY AND BOOKS,

ADAPTED FOR

Dational Schools,

&c.

SOLD BY G. ROAKE,

YORK HOUSE, 31, STRAND,

(Corner of Villiers Street.)

Best Thick Unframed Slates, all Sizes
Best Thick Framed ditto, ditto
Register Slates Framed & Ruled
Twine for Slates
Best Dutch Slate Pencils, Long and Short
Common and Best Black Lead ditto
Tin Pencil Cases
Paper Pen ditto
Ink and Ink Powders
Earthen Inkstands
• Foolscap and Post Copy Books
Ditto ditto Ciphering ditto
Slip Copies
Mounted Copy Heads
Ditto First Copies
Writing Alphabets
Stereotype Cards
Reward Tickets
Book and Card Tins
Flat and Round Rulers
Indian Rubber
Penknives and Scissars
Pens, Quills, and Pinions
Register Paper
Class Books
Admission Book
Attendance Book
Paidometer
Visitors' Book
Minutes of Committee Book
Treasurer's Account Book

NEW SCRIPT CARDS •
National School Book, No. 1
Ditto   ditto   ditto, No. 2
Sermon on the Mount
Parables
Discourses
Miracles
History of our Saviour
Ostervald's Abridgment
Chief Truths
Church Catechisms
Broken Catechisms
Collects
Arithmetical Tables
Lewis's Catechism
Crossman's Introduction
Sellon's Scripture Abridgment
Trimmer's Abridgment of the New Testament
Trimmer's Abridgment of the Old Testament
Trimmer's Scripture Catechism, Vols. I. & II.
Trimmer's Teacher's Assistant, Vols. I. & II.
Psalters
Prayer Books
Testaments
Bibles
Iremonger on Bell's System
Iremonger's Questions on the Elementary Books
Dr. Bell's Instructions
&c. &c. &c.

• *A superior edition of the* SCRIPT CARDS *is just published.*

Lightning Source UK Ltd.
Milton Keynes UK
UKOW06n0613151215

264732UK00011B/249/P